Learn DOS
—Guaranteed!
third edition

Richard P. Cadway

Windcrest®/McGraw-Hill

New York San Francisco Washington, D.C. Auckland Bogotá
Caracas Lisbon London Madrid Mexico City Milan
Montreal New Delhi San Juan Singapore
Sydney Tokyo Toronto

THIRD EDITION
FIRST PRINTING

©1993 by **Richard P. Cadway**.
Published by Windcrest Books, an imprint of TAB Books.
TAB Books is a division of McGraw-Hill, Inc.
The name "Windcrest" is a registered trademark of TAB Books.

Library of Congress Cataloging-in-Publication Data

Cadway, Richard P.
    Learn DOS—guaranteed! / by Richard Cadway.—3rd ed.
        p.   cm.
    Includes index.
    ISBN 0-8306-4331-1
    1. Operating systems (Computers)   2. PC-DOS (Computer file)   3. MS
-DOS (Computer file)   I. Title.
    QA76.76.O63C63   1993
    005.4'469—dc20   93-7050
                                                                 CIP

Editorial team: Brad Schepp, Acquisitions Editor
                Kellie Hagan, Book Editor
Production team: Katherine G. Brown, Director
                Tina M. Sourbier, Coding
                Ollie Harmon, Coding
                Sandy Hanson, Coding
                Wendy L. Small, Layout
                Donna Gladhill, Proofreading
                Jodi L. Tyler, Indexing
Design team: Jaclyn J. Boone, Designer
                Brian Allison, Associate Designer   WU1
Cover design and illustration: Sandra Blair, Harrisburg, Pa.   4351

Contents

Appendices

Acknowledgments

Many of you might not find this part of the book particularly interesting. On the other hand, those of you who see your names here will probably like this part of the book the best.

The following thanks are in order for the first edition of this book:

The first person I'd like to thank is William Klobuchar. He said to me one day, "Rick, you're really sharp working with computers. You should go into business because people need someone like you when they buy computers." Then he said, "I want to get a modem. How much are you going to charge me?" Bill has been getting his computer equipment wholesale ever since. Did I miss something? I must also thank the many people who have purchased computer systems from me. The questions they asked made me realize that a great need for this book existed.

The largest contribution to this book was made by Lawren Dowling M.Ed., who edited my writing and drew many of the illustrations in this book. She also gave me encouragement and support. Some of the photographs were taken by Richard Johnson with his special camera using 4×5 negatives. His skill and great patience enabled me to give you high-quality photos to enhance your learning without straining your eyes (save that for the monitor screen).

I'd like to thank Ed Galicki for making the CAD drawings using professional CAD programs and a plotter. Thanks also need to go to Stephen Moore (originally my acquisitions editor for Windcrest Books) for his generous help with a new author (me). Also, I thank the people at Windcrest for the opportunity to share this book with the public—and hopefully make a little money.

More thanks are in order for the second edition of *Learn DOS—Guaranteed!* Thanks again to Stephen Moore (now the network supervisor) for his suggestion and advice to do this revision. Brad Schepp, my acquisitions editor at Windcrest Books, deserves my sincerest appreciation for accepting my application for this revision. Some of the pictures were updated and a couple of new ones added. The excellent photography was done by August C. Sigur with his Bronica ETRS camera. The fine critique of the book by John Mueller (author of *The Clipper Interface Handbook* and co-author of *The Ultimate DOS Programmer's Manual* and *The Microsoft Macro Assembler 5.1*) made the first revision much easier; thank you so much John for taking the time to help me.

I owe my thanks to the quality staff of McGraw Hill/Windcrest Books and especially to Jack Nimersheim (author of *Norton pcANYWHERE: The Complete Communications Guide*) for reviewing this third edition of *Learn DOS—Guaranteed!* and giving me his knowledgeable suggestions.

Introduction

This book will introduce you to the basic DOS commands most people need in order to use their computers and run their software. The commands covered here will allow you to master the essential DOS commands that allow you to use powerful applications such as WordPerfect, Windows, Lotus 1-2-3, and dBASE.

Who should read this book

Anyone who doesn't already have a basic working knowledge of DOS should read this book. If you've just bought your first computer, you'll probably need to learn the basics of DOS. If you're using a computer at work and need to be able to copy files, make directories, back up the hard disk, and load software, you'll also need to learn DOS. Regardless of the reason, you need to understand DOS before you can use your computer effectively.

How this book is organized

Can you learn a foreign language like French by reading a French/English dictionary? Possibly, but it would be tough. DOS is similar to a foreign language and, to some people, more foreign than French. This book starts with the basics and uses repetition to help you remember the material. From there, you can go on to more advanced aspects of the language.

If you've never seen a computer before, start with Part 1, *Hardware*, to understand how the different parts of a computer operate. If you've used a computer before, I recommend that you at least skim through Part 1 for a quick review. You'll find that Part 2, *DOS Training*, is divided by commands to make it easier to both learn each command and to later find the command you want to review. Part 3, *Operations*, shows you how to make AUTOEXEC.BAT and CONFIG.SYS files, and provides basic information about loading software onto your hard drive.

What makes this book special

I've designed this book to teach you DOS in the fastest and easiest way possible. This book will give you all the necessary DOS material you need to operate your computer. I designed this approach to save you the time and drudgery often associated with using other DOS books.

Each chapter (lesson) begins with a definition and gives the DOS command. When listing the command, I've used the following standard conventions:

- The command name is in all caps.
- Any variable information (like *filename* or *directory*) is in lowercase italic.
- Any optional information (like switches or parameters) are enclosed in square brackets, [ ].

Each chapter then continues with a list of things you should already know and then provides practice. When I touch upon an important topic, you'll find a page number directly after it so you can conveniently review that topic before going on. You'll also notice a constant review of previous material as you progress through the book.

Whenever information you need to type on the keyboard appears on a line by itself in the book, it will have a gray screen behind it so you can easily find it on the page or in a chapter. When the prompt (like **C:\>**) is shown in the text, it will be in bold, also so you can easily and quickly recognize it.

  Occasionally you'll see icons or symbols in the margin. Two kinds of icons are used in this book. The icon of a hand with a string tied around a finger indicates something you should remember. The icon of the pair of eyes looking at the text indicates something to watch out for.

Hardware & software requirements

Because most computers these days are sold with a hard-disk drive, I'm going to assume that you have an IBM or IBM-compatible computer with one or two floppy drives, and a hard-disk drive of the letter designation C.

Most of the examples in this book are from MS-DOS versions 3.3, 5.0, and 6.0 . The DOS message wording varies from version to version, but the concepts should be interchangeable. If you're using a DOS version such as 1.0, 1.1, 2.0, or 2.1, now is a good time to upgrade to DOS 6.0.

If you purchased your computer system by mail order, your hard drive might need to be partitioned and formatted, so I've included information in Appendix A on partitioning and formatting. If you purchased your system from a local dealer, your hard drive probably has been partitioned, formatted, and contains a \DOS directory.

It's important to follow this book from beginning to end because each chapter builds upon the previous chapter. I've omitted all the unnecessary details and included only what's necessary for you to learn DOS in the simplest and easiest way.

I guarantee you'll learn from this book or your money back.

Part one
Hardware

1 The basic computer system

There are many different brands of computer systems on the market. Like cars, some are engineered better than others. I've found that popular computer magazines accurately evaluate most computer products and can help you to make a smart purchase.

At the present time, most computer systems being sold have the following minimum equipment: an 80386-SX microprocessor, a 40-megabyte hard drive, a high-density 5¼-inch and/or 3½-inch floppy drive, and 1 megabyte of RAM.

Computer-system requirements

I would recommend a system with an 80386-DX or more powerful microprocessor, 4 megabytes of RAM, a super VGA video card and monitor, and a 130-megabyte hard drive. Because higher-capacity hard drives and higher-density RAM memory chips are becoming more affordable, software developers are writing programs that require more disk storage space and occupy more RAM (random-access memory).

The reason MS-DOS 5.0 and 6.0 are so popular is that you can load the system files and a number of TSRs (terminate-and-stay-resident, or memory-resident programs, p. 44) into the HMA (high-memory area, p. 41), and still have about 600K of RAM available to run application software such as WordPerfect or Lotus 1-2-3. Hard-drive size is limited only by the amount of money you have to spend. If you get a hard drive that's too small, however, you'll have to transfer your software from the hard drive to floppy disks and back again. This process can be very inconvenient and time-consuming.

Computer-system components

Figure 1-1 shows the major parts of a typical '386/'486 computer. Following are descriptions of the most widely used parts:

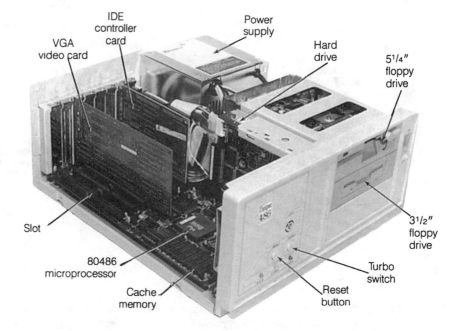

1-1
The internal components of a typical computer.

Microprocessor

The microprocessor in FIG. 1-1 is an 80486-50 Intel chip. It's the most expensive part of this computer.

Power supply

The typical power supply has a dual-input voltage switch, with which you can select either 110 or 220 volts. This switch is frequently covered with a piece of tape so you don't accidentally change the setting. There are usually six power connectors. Two of these connectors have six pins each that plug into the main computer board, with the black wires facing each other. The other connectors are used to power the floppy and hard drives.

Floppy drive

The floppy drive reads and writes data to a floppy disk. Having both a 5¼-inch and 3½-inch drive enables you to use disks from practically any IBM-compatible machine. If your computer has a hard drive, the main purpose of the floppy drive is to add and remove data from your hard drive. If you don't have a hard drive, the floppy drive is then used to run programs.

Hard drive

The hard drive, because of its large capacity, can store many programs. It's at least 10 times as fast as a floppy drive when reading and writing data. Also, there's no need to change disks as when using a floppy drive.

The memory chips make up the random-access memory (RAM). *RAM* is the work space used when you're running a program. RAM memory is available in DRAM (dynamic RAM) chips, SIMMs (straight-inline memory modules), and SIP (straight-inline with pins) modules, as shown in FIG. 1-2. A DRAM chip is a single dynamic-RAM memory chip. A SIMM consists of a printed circuit board with DRAM chips soldered to it, with a row of contacts along one edge. A SIP is similar to a SIMM except it has a row of pins that plug into the row of holes in a socket instead of a row of contacts like the SIMM.

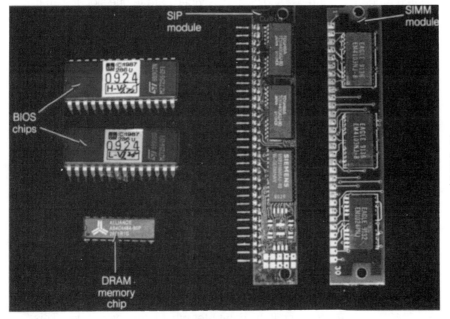

1-2
A pair of BIOS chips, DRAM chips, and SIP and SIMM modules.

In older computers, there are typically 36 DRAM sockets that, when filled with 256K chips, give one megabyte of RAM. Filling 18 sockets with 256K chips and the remaining 18 sockets with 64K chips will give you 640K RAM. In newer computers, four 256K SIMMs or SIPs equal one megabyte of RAM, four 1-meg SIMMs or SIPs equal four megabytes of RAM, and four 4-meg SIMMs or SIPs equal 16 megabytes of RAM. The speed at which memory chips can operate is rated in nanoseconds (abbreviated *ns*). An 80ns chip is faster than a 100ns chip. The amount of memory must be fast enough for the speed of the computer or the system will lock up.

Cache memory consists of a small (64–256K) number of very fast (15–35ns) memory chips. When something is read from normal memory (at 60–80ns), a copy is made in the cache memory. When the same data is required again, the data is read from the very fast cache memory, which makes the computer run faster.

BIOS chips The BIOS chips shown in FIG. 1-2 are read-only memory chips and function as the basic input/output system (abbreviated as *BIOS*) for the computer. Some of the best known brands are Award, Phoenix, DTK, and AMI. Modern BIOS chips contain a CMOS setup routine. Older computers use a matched pair of BIOS chips (low and high or odd and even), but modern computers usually have one large-capacity BIOS chip (p. 36).

Slots Slots let you expand your computer system by adding cards that perform a desired function. Figure 1-1 shows a VGA video card in one slot and an IDE hard- and floppy-drive controller card in another slot. There are connectors on the main computer board that line up with openings in the back of the case. The combination of an opening and a connector is considered to be a slot.

Controller card The typical controller card transfers data using the floppy and hard drives. These cards usually control two floppy drives and two hard drives. MFM, RLL, SCSI, ESDI, and IDE are the different types of driver cards, with the IDE being the least expensive and most popular. The IDE controller card in FIG. 1-1 has built in parallel, serial, and game ports.

Turbo & reset switches Many computers, like the one in FIG. 1-1, have a turbo switch to change the operating speed of the computer, and a reset switch to cold-boot the system without having to turn off the main power. Some computers allow you to change the operating speed by pushing a combination of keys on the keyboard.

Running SETUP In the '286, '386, and '486 computer, setting up the CMOS is accomplished by either a program in the BIOS chips or by using a floppy disk that contains a CMOS SETUP program. Besides allowing you to change the time and date, the CMOS SETUP lets you tell the computer what equipment it has. This might sound strange, but when the computer begins to boot up (start running), it looks at the setup information and proceeds to check its memory, drives, interrupts, etc., to be sure everything is operating properly.

You can invoke most CMOS SETUP routines by holding down the Alt and Ctrl keys and hitting the Escape key. Some CMOS SETUPs can be accessed at any time, and some only during boot time. There are many different ways to begin SETUP programs in the BIOS because there are many different brands of BIOS. I suggest that you look at your computer-operation booklet to find the method your computer uses to access the CMOS SETUP program.

The CMOS SETUP information is held in a CMOS memory chip (p. 136). This chip requires a constant source of electricity to maintain this information, which is why all '286, '386, and '486 computer boards have a nicad battery with a charging circuit or an external battery pack. Your computer could lose its SETUP if the battery fails or if your power supply sends out a voltage spike. If your computer loses its SETUP, your system won't be harmed nor will you loose data from your hard drive, but your system won't operate until the information is restored. The following is a typical CMOS SETUP routine:

```
DATE                     01/05/89
TIME                     14:14:00
DISKETTE 1   (A)         1.2
DISKETTE 2   (B)         1.44
FIXED DISK 1 (C)         3
FIXED DISK 2 (D)         NONE
VIDEO TYPE               VGA
BASE MEMORY SIZE         640
EXTENDED MEMORY SIZE     384
SPEED SELECTION          HIGH SPEED

    Save Current Options [Y/N]?
```

Let's go through all of this information to understand what each entry is for.

DATE   This sets the date in the calendar.

TIME   This sets the time in the clock.

DISKETTE 1 (A)   This is drive A: and is usually a 1.2Mb or a 1.44Mb high-density floppy drive, but can be a 360K or 720K floppy drive.

DISKETTE 2 (B)   This is drive B: and is usually a 360K or 1.44Mb floppy drive, but can be a 1.2Mb or 720K floppy drive.

DISK 1 (C)   If you have one hard drive, this is it. It's very important to know the type (number) for your drive. The type you use tells the computer the number of cylinders, heads, and sectors per track, plus other necessary information. Be sure you have the correct drive-type number. Some CMOS SETUPs have a user-definable hard-drive type, which enables you to use any type of hard drive by directly entering the drive-type information.

DISK 2 (D)   If you have two hard drives, this is the second drive. Again, be sure you know the correct hard-drive type.

VIDEO TYPE   This informs the system whether you have a color or monochrome video adapter card. There's usually a jumper (p. 41) on the main computer board that also needs to be set. Consult your manual.

BASE MEMORY   This will be either 512 or 640.

EXTENDED MEMORY   This will be 0 if your system has 640K of RAM. If you have one megabyte of RAM, it should be 384 (1024–640 = 384). Modify this entry in relation to the amount of memory you add. Your computer's main board might have jumpers or switches to configure the memory, so consult your computer manual if you add memory.

SPEED SELECT This automatically selects slow or fast CPU (p. 137) speed upon system startup.

Save Current Options [Y/N]? Pressing the Y key will save the information and begin booting. Pressing the N key will restore previous information and begin booting.

Disk drives & floppy disks

The disk drives in your computer system are used to store and transfer data. The two major types of drives are the hard drive and the floppy drive. The following is information you should already know:

- The CMOS SETUP is stored in a memory chip that needs a constant source of electricity, which is supplied by a battery (p. 16).
- '286, '386, and '486 computers know what equipment they have by checking the CMOS SETUP data.
- Slots are used to expand the computer system (p. 16).
- RAM is made up of DRAM memory chips, SIMMs, and/or SIP modules on the main computer board (p. 15).
- RAM is the computer's work space (p. 15).

What you should already know

A tape recorder changes sounds to magnetic pulses and records them on a tape. Likewise, floppy- and hard-disk drives change letters into magnetic pulses and record them on a disk. To retrieve data, disk drives read the magnetic pulses from the disks and convert them back into characters, the way a tape recorder reads the magnetic pulses from the tape and converts them back into sounds.

Disk-drive operation

The hard-disk drive

The *hard-disk drive* (also called a *hard drive* or *fixed-disk drive*) is a mass-storage device that allows you to store many programs and files for quick access. The hard drive saves and retrieves data at least 10 times faster than a floppy drive. The most common hard drives range from 40 to 250 megabytes in capacity.

The term *fixed disk* comes from the fact that the disk in a hard drive isn't removable like a floppy disk, but fixed in a permanent location. The term *hard disk* comes from the fact that the disk in the hard drive is rigid and not flexible like a 5¼-inch floppy disk. Older hard drives are typically 5¼ inch, either full or half height. Newer hard drives are typically 3½ inch, either standard or 1-inch height.

Hard drives can be physical or logical. Suppose you had a 120-megabyte hard drive. If it was formatted with DOS 4.01 or later, you could have a 120-megabyte drive C: and therefore one physical drive of the drive-letter designation C:. Now suppose you bought your computer before DOS 4.01 was available. You would be using DOS 3.30, and therefore be limited to partitions of 32 megabytes. This means that the maximum size of drive C: would be 32 megabytes. So what about the rest of the hard disk's capacity? DOS 3.30 gives you the ability to divide the drive into different logical-drive letters, so your 120-megabyte drive would consist of one physical drive and the logical drive letters of C, D, E, and F. Each drive letter would contain 32Mg and behave as a separate physical drive.

The hard drive in FIG. 2-1 contains four hard disks, commonly referred to as platters. Although only one magnetic head is shown, there's usually one on each side of each platter, for a total of eight heads. Either a stepping motor or a voice coil is used to position the magnetic heads over the platters to read and write data. A motor on the underside spins the hard disks at a constant high speed. The high speed makes the heads float on a cushion of air above the platters, so there's no contact and therefore no wear.

Most modern hard drives that contain a voice coil also auto-park the heads. Auto-park typically involves moving the heads to the end of the disk and physically holding them up, thereby preventing contact with the platters when the disk stops spinning and the cushion of air is gone. Most older drives that use stepping motors don't park the heads, so it's a good idea to use a program like PARK.COM to park the heads before you move the computer. A commonly asked question is, "After I park the drive, do I have to unpark it?" The answer is no. All drives resume normal operation when the computer is turned on.

The floppy-disk drive

The *floppy-disk drive*, also called just the *floppy drive*, is mainly used to put programs on or take programs off the hard drive, although it can be used to run programs as well. These are four major categories of floppy drives:

- 5¼-inch 360K capacity
- 5¼-inch 1.2-megabyte capacity (high density)

- 3½-inch 720K capacity
- 3½-inch 1.44-megabyte capacity (high density)

The PS/2 line of IBM computers uses 3½-inch floppy drives exclusively. Most IBM-compatible computers are available with any combination of 5¼-inch and 3½-inch floppy drives.

2-1
A 3½-inch, 1-inch high hard drive with its cover removed.

Voice coil

Magnetic head

Platters

Seagate Technology

Floppy disks

Floppy disks, also called *floppy diskettes*, are used in floppy drives and are inexpensive and easy to transport. They're ideal for moving and copying programs and files from one computer to another.

Figure 2-2 shows the two most common types of floppy disks. The small size and shield that protects the internal disk are the main advantages of the 3½-inch diskettes. The major advantage of the 5¼-inch disk is its lower cost.

5¼-inch disks

The two major types of 5¼-inch floppy disks are the 360K, double-sided, double-density (also called *low-density*) disk and the 1.2Mb high-density disk.

The 360K DSDD disks can hold 362,496 bytes of data. You'll find that most software you buy will come on 360K disks; the reason being that they can be read by either an XT-compatible machine, which usually has only 360K drives, or a '286, '386, or '486 computer, which usually has a 1.2Mb drive.

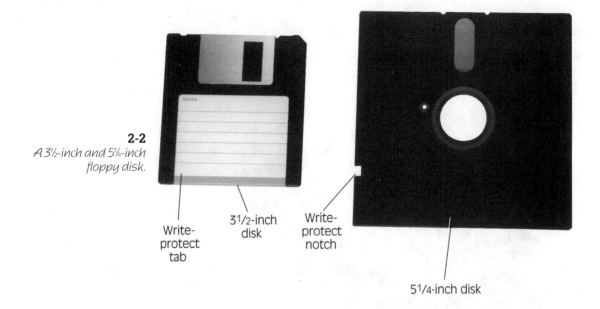

2-2
A 3½-inch and 5¼-inch floppy disk.

Write-
protect
tab

3½-inch
disk

Write-
protect
notch

5¼-inch disk

The 5¼-inch, 1.2Mb, high-density disk looks identical to a 360K DSDD disk, but they're actually quite different. IBM developed the high-density floppy drive and high-density disks for their IBM-AT computers because a faster and easier method was needed for backing up the larger-capacity AT hard drives.

High-density disks are rotated faster than 360K disks, and the data spots that are written to the disk are closer together, requiring the use of a higher-grade magnetic coating. A high-density disk will hold 1,213,952 bytes of data, which is approximately 3.3 times that of a 360K disk. Therefore, if it takes 20 high-density disks to back up a hard drive, then it would take 66 360K DSDD disks. Hooray for high-density disks!

3½-inch disks The 3½-inch, 720K, double-sided, double-density (DSDD) disk (again, called *low-density*) can hold 730,112 bytes of data. The 3½-inch, 1.44Mb, high-density disk can hold 1,449,984 bytes of data.

Disk insertion Figure 2-3 shows how to insert a 5¼-inch disk into its drive. Make sure the notch is on the left side and the lever is in the up position, as shown. When the disk is all the way in, pivot the lever in a clockwise motion to a downward position.

If the notch in the left side of the disk is covered, the computer won't write any information (data) to the disk. This is called *write protect*. Most disks on the market come with a sheet of adhesive paper rectangles called *write-protect tabs*. To ensure that the data on the disk isn't accidentally erased,

Lever

Notch

2-3
Proper insertion of a 5¼-inch disk.

simply fold a tab over the notch. Remove the tab when you want to copy data to the disk.

Make sure the label is facing up and the write protect tab is on the left side when you insert a 3½-inch disk into its floppy drive. The 3½-inch disk has a built-in plastic write-protect tab that slides back and forth into either an open or a closed position. When the tab is in the open position, no data can be written to or erased from the disk. The closed position (when the opening is covered) is for normal read and write operations.

3 The keyboard & mouse

The two most common types of keyboards are the 84-key (standard AT) and the 101-key (enhanced) keyboards. All software programs require the use of an input device like a keyboard or mouse.

What you should already know

- The cursor is the blinking light (usually an underscore or box) on the monitor (computer screen) that indicates where the next character will appear.
- Slots enable computer expansion by accepting cards (p. 6).
- 5¼-inch floppy disks are either DSDD or high density (p. 11).
- 3½-inch floppy disks are smaller and have a protective shield (p. 12).

The 84-key keyboard

Figure 3-1 shows the 84-key keyboard and location of frequently used keys. The Alt and Ctrl keys are used in conjunction with other keys. For example, if you hold down the Ctrl key and strike the letter C, you'll send a break signal to the computer (p. 35) If you hold down both the Ctrl and Alt keys and strike the Delete key, you'll tell the computer to do a warm boot (p. 144). Holding down the Shift key and striking the PrtSc (print screen) key will cause everything showing on the monitor to be copied to the printer (don't do this unless your printer is online).

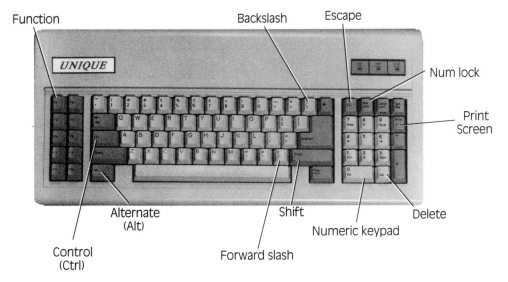

Function · Backslash · Escape · Num lock · Print Screen · Alternate (Alt) · Shift · Delete · Control (Ctrl) · Forward slash · Numeric keypad

3-1 *A typical 84-key keyboard.*

I personally find the 84-key keyboard easier to use with programs like WordPerfect because of the proximity of the function keys to the Alt and Ctrl keys. You can use one hand to easily pick any combination of these keys. A disadvantage of the 84-key keyboard is that you must push the Num Lock key each time you switch from using numbers on the numeric keypad to using the arrow keys.

The 101-key keyboard, shown in FIG. 3-2, shows the location of frequently used keys as well as the cursor keypad, which the 84-key keyboard doesn't have. The greatest advantage of the 101-key keyboard over the 84-key keyboard is that you can enter numbers and use the arrow keys without having to press the Num Lock key. For this reason, if you're going to use a spreadsheet program like Lotus 1-2-3, I recommend the 101 keyboard. The 101 keyboard also has 12 function keys compared to 10 on the 84-key keyboard, and some software packages assign operations to the new function keys F11 and F12.

The 101-key keyboard

Most keyboards for IBM-compatible computers use a five-pin DIN connector, like the one in FIG 3-3, for connecting the keyboard to the computer. The key helps you align the plug for correct insertion into the socket, which is usually located in a round or oval hole in the back of the computer.

There's an electrical, not a visible, difference between the keyboards used on XT (8088) and AT-class ('286, '386, and '486) computers. Some keyboards have switches on the bottom that need to be set to XT or AT in order to work correctly. Some keyboards can automatically sense which type of computer

Electrical compatibility

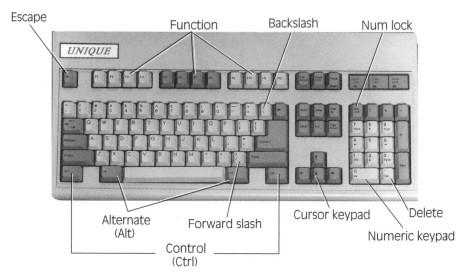

Escape   Function   Backslash   Num lock

UNIQUE

Alternate   Forward slash   Cursor keypad   Delete
(Alt)
Control   Numeric keypad
(Ctrl)

3-2 *A typical 101-key enhanced keyboard.*

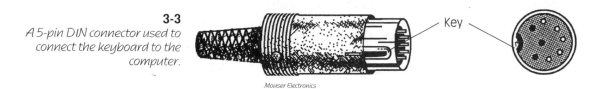

3-3

A 5-pin DIN connector used to connect the keyboard to the computer.

Key

Mouser Electronics

they're connected to and automatically switch to that type of computer. Then there are others that are strictly for an XT or AT and aren't interchangeable. You can't hurt the computer by using the wrong keyboard, but you'll get an error message and the computer won't operate.

Keyboard tips

It's important to have a high-quality keyboard because you'll be using it so much. Some cheap keyboards have keys that get loose and spongy after a short time and others have keys that are stiff and tend to stick. If you don't already have one, insist on a keyboard of high quality.

The mouse

The *mouse* is an input device that moves the cursor (usually an arrow or box) on the screen in the same direction that you move the mouse. A ball on the underside of the mouse rolls when you move the mouse across the tabletop, and gives the computer the data it needs to move the cursor. You use the buttons on the mouse to select images on the monitor that you point to with the cursor.

Some mice have two buttons, and some have three buttons, like the one in FIG. 3-4. Some software programs will use all three buttons and some programs only two buttons. The mouse in FIG. 3-4 is a serial mouse and has a 9-pin D connector attached to its cable. Also in FIG. 3-4 is a 9-to-25-pin converter, which will let you use this mouse with the 25-pin serial port on your computer. The bus mouse in FIG. 3-5 operates like the serial mouse. It has a round connector instead of the 9-pin D connector, and plugs into its own driver card that you insert into one of the slots in your computer.

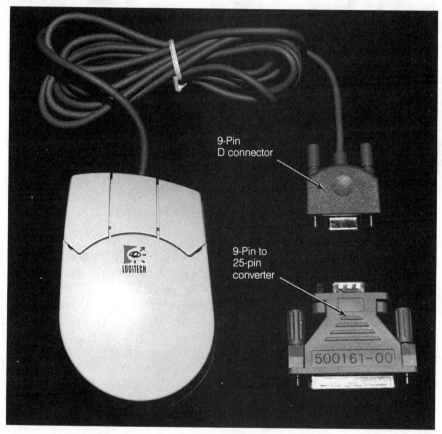

9-Pin
D connector

9-Pin to
25-pin
converter

LOGITECH

500161-00

3-4
A three-button serial mouse and 9-to-25-pin converter.

MS-DOS supports only two external serial ports. The typical computer has five to eight slots. Selecting a serial or bus mouse depends on what equipment you have and what you plan to do with the system in the future. Let's look at a couple of examples:

Serial vs. bus

Example 1 Your system has four open slots and one available serial port. You plan on buying a printer with a serial interface. You already have an internal modem and don't plan to use any more slots. Because the price of the serial and bus mouse is about the same, I would pick the bus mouse.

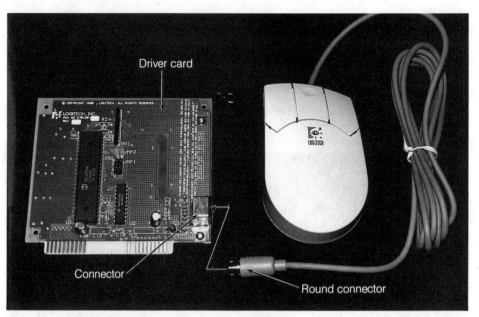

3-5 *A three-button bus mouse and driver card.*

With four open slots and no plans to use them, and only one or two serial ports, the bus mouse is the wiser choice.

Example 2 Your system has two open slots and two serial ports, and you plan to buy a printer with a parallel interface (the most common interface). You also have another computer in your office with a serial port. I would pick a serial mouse over the bus mouse in this situation. First of all, the system has only two open slots and, when the slots are full, there's no more room for expansion. Second, you have two serial ports and aren't using them. Third, the serial mouse is easy to connect to another computer; simply plug it into the serial port and load the mouse-driver software. Attaching the bus mouse to another computer requires removing both computer covers and moving the bus-driver card from one computer to the other. You then have to replace the covers and load the mouse-driver software.

The clock & calendar

The time and date are important factors in our personal and business activities and also to the activities of your computer system. Having a built-in clock and calendar frees us from having to remember to enter the time and date.

Why have a clock & calendar?

DOS records the TIME and DATE with each file that is created and uses this information when you execute the BACKUP, MSBACKUP (MS-DOS 6.0) and RESTORE commands. Some programs use the clock and calendar to record when data entries were made and sort data records chronologically. Other programs use the clock and calendar to allow access to computer networks only on predetermined days and times. And still others use the clock and calendar to put the DATE and TIME on invoices and other documents automatically.

Programs like Lotus 1-2-3 allow you to TIME and DATE stamp your spreadsheets using special commands that read your computer's clock and calendar. And don't forget, your computer can also be used as a $1,500.00 desk clock.

What you should already know

- Booting the computer means turning on or resetting the computer (p. 6).
- The blinking light (usually an underscore) on the monitor is called the *cursor* (p. 14).
- You can buy a serial mouse or a bus mouse (p. 17).

- The basic keyboards are the 84-key (AT) and the 101-key (enhanced) keyboards (p. 14).
- The command DATE will show the current date and ask for a change. The command TIME will show the current time and ask for a change.

Entering the time & date

If you don't have an AUTOEXEC.BAT file in the \ROOT directory of drive C:, DOS will always ask you to enter the TIME and DATE. Boot your computer by inserting your DOS system disk into drive A: and then turning on the computer (or, if your system files are contained on your hard drive, just turning on the computer). You'll be asked to enter the new date:

```
Current DATE is Tue 1-01-1980
Enter new DATE (mm-dd-yy):
```

If the current date is incorrect, you can enter the new date in the format shown and hit the Enter key. If the current date shown is correct, just hit the Enter key to keep it. You'll then be asked to enter the new time:

```
Current TIME is 0:03:31.24
Enter new TIME:
```

If the current time is incorrect, enter the new time in 24-hour format and hit the Enter key. If the current time is correct, just hit the Enter key to keep it. Then you'll see the copyright, DOS version number, and prompt. The prompt should be either **A>** or **C>**.

Note: If you type in a new date or time, the information you type will be loaded into computer memory and used until you turn off the system, unless you're using MS-DOS 3.3 or later on a '286, '386, or '486 computer. I haven't seen an AT-type computer yet that hasn't had a clock and calendar built into the main computer board.

The clock in XT compatibles

If you have an XT-compatible (8088) computer, you might not have a clock and calendar at all. The clock and calendar usually come on a card with the floppy-disk controller, game, parallel and serial ports, and is called a multi-I/O (input/output) card. In some computers, the clock and calendar might be on a card all by itself. Normally, the card containing the clock and calendar comes with the necessary software to set the clock. For example, I've used the multi-I/O card to install a program called TIMER.COM in the directory \TIMER. Then I used the AUTOEXEC.BAT file to call the TIMER.COM program located in the \TIMER directory to copy the correct time and date into computer memory. To set the time and date on an XT, follow the instructions provided with your clock and calendar card.

5 Parallel & serial ports

Parallel and serial ports allow the exchange of data between the computer and external devices. Some of the external devices that can be connected to these ports are the printer, mouse, external modem, networking cables, and data-acquisition equipment. The terms *parallel interface* and *serial interface* are used when describing the type of connection available on an external device.

A *port* is a gateway. A port allows the passage of data in the form of electrical pulses to and from an external device. The parallel port in a computer is simply a long D-shaped object with 25 holes, containing electrical contacts. It's called a female D connector. The serial port is like the parallel port except is has 25 pins instead of holes and is called a male D connector. There's also a 9-pin serial port that performs the same function, but has the advantage of being smaller than the 25-pin serial port. Another name for serial port is *COM port*. The first serial port is COM1 and the second serial port is COM2. COM is an abbreviation for *communication*.

- The keyboard has a five-pin DIN connector to connect it to the computer (p. 15).
- You can add cards to the slots in a computer in order to expand it (p. 16).
- Most XT-type computers use a card in a slot to add a clock and calendar to the computer system (p. 20).

What you should already know

- AT-class ('286, '386, and '486) computers typically have the clock and calendar built into the main computer board (p. 20).
- Parallel and serial ports are typically located on the back of the computer.
- Parallel and serial interfaces are used to connect external devices to parallel and serial ports on the computer.

Port identification

Looking at FIG. 5-1, you can see that the serial, parallel, and monitor ports are all elongated, D-shaped connectors. The D shape allows the mating connector to be inserted in only one way. The gender of the connector helps prevent you from plugging a device into the wrong type of port.

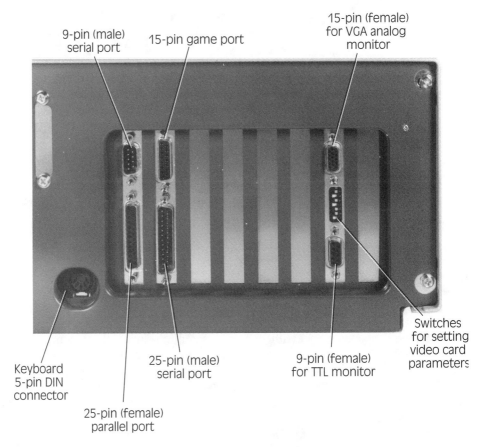

5-1 *The back panel of a computer, showing its various ports.*

If you look back at FIG. 3-4 in chapter 3, you'll see that the mouse's 9-pin D connector can plug into the 9-pin serial port shown in FIG. 5-1, and the 9-to-25-pin adapter shown in FIG. 3-4 can be used to plug the mouse into the 25-pin serial port shown in FIG. 5-1. The 15-pin game port shown in FIG. 5-1 allows you to connect a joystick controller to the computer and is used mainly for playing video games. The parallel port is the 25-pin female D connector shown in FIG. 5-1 and, because it's the only parallel port on this computer, it would be the primary port, LPT1. DOS allows you to use up to three parallel ports in one computer; they're referred to as LPT1, LPT2, and LPT3.

The computer shown in FIG. 5-1 is equipped with a VGA adapter, which has a 15-pin female D connector and a 9-pin female D connector. The 15-pin female connector will accept only a VGA (Video Graphics Array) analog monitor cable or a multisync-type monitor with a special adapter cable. The 9-pin female connector will accept TTL monitors; use the switches to select which TTL monitor will be connected. TTL monitors are typically monochrome, RGB, and EGA-type monitors and require digital input.

The video adapter

Usually, on a monochrome video card, the connector either above or below the monitor's 9-pin connector is the primary parallel port, or LPT1, and any other parallel ports would be LPT2 and LPT3. DOS will recognize up to three parallel ports in one computer. Plug the appropriate connector of the printer cable into LPT1.

The parallel port moves data along parallel lines, which are the wires in the printer cable. Imagine a freeway with eight lanes going in each direction. It's rush hour and the cars are bumper to bumper (not hard to visualize, is it?) and there's a toll booth for each lane. Eight cars pull into the eight toll booths and, when signaled, all eight cars are allowed to pass through at the same time. Each time the toll booths are signaled, another eight cars pass through. In the computer world, each group of eight cars represents a byte, equal to one character. This is how parallel ports send characters to a parallel printer.

Parallel & serial data transfer

The serial port moves data in a straight line. Imagine a road with one lane in each direction. Again, the cars are bumper to bumper. There's one toll booth on the east bound lane and the toll-booth worker counts eight cars and then rubber stamps the word *stop* on the ninth car. Then he counts another eight cars and stamps the word *stop* on the ninth car, and continues this process until there are no more cars. A computer would consider each group of eight cars to be one byte (character) and the cars with the word *stop* stamped on them are called stop bits and would be used to separate the bytes.

Most printers come with a parallel interface, which means you connect them to the parallel port on the computer with a parallel printer cable. Some expensive programs won't operate unless a security device, called a *key*, is plugged into the parallel port.

When to use a parallel port

You would use a parallel port for a plotter with a parallel interface, although only a very small number of plotters have a parallel interface. There are available programs, such as LapLink and FastLinx, that enable you to transfer files back and forth between two computers by connecting a special cable to the parallel ports of each computer. Use the parallel port to communicate with a laser printer. Most laser printers have both a serial and a parallel interface, but are connected in parallel because it's easier.

When to use a serial (RS-232) port

Some printers come with a serial interface, and many offer a serial-interface option. Use the serial interface when you need greater communication control, or when communicating in both directions. Most plotters require a serial-port connection.

You must use a serial port with a serial mouse and an external modem. Some inexpensive networks use serial ports to connect one computer to another one so they can communicate back and forth. Digitizer tablets use a serial port for input to the computer in a manner similar to that of a mouse.

The serial cable shown on the left in FIG. 5-2 is a 25-pin female to 25-pin male. The serial cable shown on the right in FIG. 5-2 is a 9-pin female to 25-pin male. Which cable you use is determined by the type of serial-port connectors you have available on your computer. Some serial devices require specially jumpered cables to operate correctly. These devices usually come with diagrams showing the correct jumpering, but you'll most likely need to know how to solder in order to alter the cable.

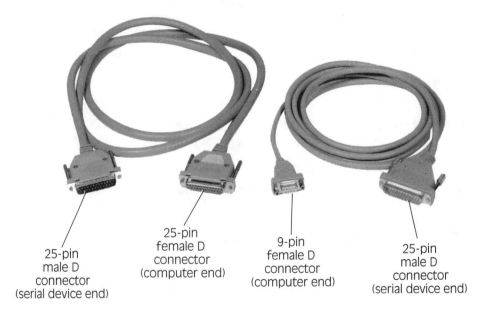

25-pin male D connector (serial device end)

25-pin female D connector (computer end)

9-pin female D connector (computer end)

25-pin male D connector (serial device end)

5-2 *Two types of serial cables.*

If your computer has two parallel ports (25-pin female connectors), you need to know which one is the primary port. If you have a monochrome monitor, you most likely have a 25-pin female D connector (parallel port) above or below the 9-pin female monitor connector, which is the primary parallel port, LPT1. The other parallel port is LPT2. If you have a color monitor and more than one parallel port, you need to connect the printer to one of the ports and send a test print file to LPT1. If no printing occurs, plug the cable into the other parallel port (LPT2) and try the same print procedure.

Identifying the first parallel port

The parallel interface connection is simpler than the serial connection. You simply plug in the cable, configure the software for parallel operation (LPT1), and away you go.

Serial vs. parallel

The serial (RS-232) interface, on the other hand, is more complicated, but offers more control of what, how, and when data is transferred. The computer and the printer (device) must be set up to operate at the same speed (baud rate), with the correct parity, the correct number of data bits, and the correct number of stop bits or there will be no communication.

There are many reasons to use serial over parallel. First of all, it isn't recommended that a parallel cable be over 30 feet in length, but a serial cable can be up to a 100 feet and, in some circumstances, longer. Second, the serial cable can use as few as two wires to transfer data, in comparison to the parallel cable, which requires a minimum of 11 wires. Third, the serial interface is designed to communicate in both directions whereas the parallel interface is usually used to transfer data only in one direction.

6 Connecting the printer

The two ways to connect a printer are parallel and serial. (See chapter 5 for more information on parallel and serial ports.) Most printers are connected in parallel because it's the easiest, fastest, and least expensive interface to use.

What you should already know

- A computer can have both serial and parallel ports (p. 22).
- Serial communication usually transfers data in both directions.
- Parallel ports normally transfer data in one direction, from the computer to the printer.
- A parallel port has a 25-pin female connector (p. 23).
- A serial port has either a 25-pin or 9-pin male connector (p. 24).
- The most popular serial-port specification is RS-232.
- COM1 is another name for serial port number 1.

The parallel interface

Most printers come with a parallel interface and are considered output devices, which means that they accept data only from your computer. Because the parallel interface was designed only to output data and requires no user intervention, it's ideal for most printer applications.

Parallel cable-to-printer connection

Parallel printers have a connector on their back or side, called a Centronics interface. The name Centronics originated from the company that started using this type of interface, and was accepted as a standard by the computer industry.

The Centronics connector on the printer shown in FIG. 6-1 has 36 electrical contacts and a D shape so the plug can be inserted only one way. There are also two spring clips, one on each side of the printer connector, which snap over the cable connector to hold it in place. To connect the cable to the printer, insert the Centronics cable connector into the printer connector and snap the clips over it.

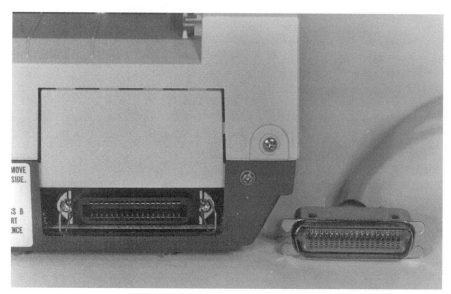

6-1
The Centronics connectors of a printer and a printer cable.

The parallel port of a computer has a 25-pin female D connector. The typical printer cable has a 25-pin male connector on one end that plugs into the parallel port on the computer.

Parallel cable-to-computer connection

A serial printer isn't as easy to connect to a computer as a parallel printer mainly because there are parameters that need to be set and because not all serial cables are the same. Whole books have been written about serial communication, which should give you some idea as to how complicated this subject can get. I'll describe only the most typical computer-to-serial-printer connection in this book.

The serial interface

The first thing you need to do is review the instruction manual that comes with your serial printer. Look for the serial-communication parameters, which will probably be the same as the commonly used parameters shown in FIG. 6-2. You must use the parameters in the manual for proper communication. The manual should also give you a diagram and specifications of the proper cable to be used. Ask your dealer if you aren't sure which cable to use. Connect the serial cable by inserting the 25-pin male connector of the cable into the 25-pin female connector on the printer.

The printer's serial interface

```
        ┌──── Baud rate
        │ ┌──── Parity
        │ │ ┌──── Number of data bits
        │ │ │ ┌──── Number of stop bits
       9600 N 8 1
```

6-2

A description of commonly used serial parameters.

The computer's serial port

Connect the 25-pin female connector of the serial cable to either of the serial ports (COM1 or COM2) of the computer. You can set the serial-port communication parameters with the DOS MODE command. The following command statement sets COM1 at 9600 baud, no parity, eight data bits, and one stop bit.

```
MODE COM1:96,N,8,1
```

If you're using a word-processing program like WordPerfect 5.1, you don't need to use the DOS MODE command. The program automatically sets the serial parameters and communication port when you select your printer.

Types of printers

There are many types of printers, the most common being a dot-matrix printer. An advantage of a dot-matrix printer is that it can print text and graphics on the same page. It also prints faster than daisywheel printers. The majority of dot-matrix printers have either 9 or 24 pins. A 24-pin printer will produce higher-quality output, but also costs more money.

The daisywheel printer is often referred to as a letter-quality printer. It uses a print wheel like many electric typewriters, and operates in much the same way. It has the advantage of letter-quality output, but it's noisy, prints slowly, and is unable to print graphics.

A laser printer is basically a dry-paper copying machine, which uses a laser to write data to the copying drum. A laser printer can produce text and graphics on the same page and gives a much higher-quality output than dot-matrix printers. The disadvantage of a laser printer is its high cost of operation and inability to make carbon copies like a dot matrix or daisywheel printer.

As with most purchases, select a printer that best suits your needs— weighing both the price and quality factors.

7 *Basic operation*

In order to understand the basic operation of a typical computer system, it's important to know how the different components of the system interact with each other.

These are the important events that take place when you *boot up* (turn on) a computer system:

When you turn on the computer

1. You turn on the computer.
2. Electricity goes to the main computer board.
3. The BIOS instructs the computer to run tests.
4. The keyboard is tested.
5. The RAM is tested.
6. The first floppy drive and then the second (if there is one) are tested.
7. The hard disk is tested.
8. If all the tests are okay, the BIOS instructs the first floppy drive to load the DOS system.
9. If the system files aren't found on the disk in drive A: (or if there's no disk in drive A: at all), then the BIOS looks at hard drive C: for the system files.
10. When the system files are found, they're loaded into memory. Now DOS is capable of controlling the computer.

You've booted the computer, and DOS is now in control of the computer system. All functions are controlled by DOS whether you're accessing the

DOS operation

disk drives, sending a file to the printer, accepting input from the keyboard, or loading software into memory.

If you enter the DIR command to check drive C: for files, DOS will execute the command and list the files on the monitor. Then it waits for the next command to be entered.

Processing data

The microprocessor, or CPU (central processing unit) does all the number crunching by manipulating the data in memory. Microprocessor chips can be identified by their numbers, like 8088, 80286, 80386, and 80486. The math coprocessor is much more efficient than the microprocessor for doing high-level math, so the microprocessor sends all the math it can to the coprocessor. This can increase computing speed up to 600%. Math coprocessor chips are identified by the numbers 8087, 80287, and 80387. The 80486DX microprocessor has a built-in 80487 math coprocessor, but the 80486SX microprocessor doesn't.

Data flow through the computer

Characters you type into a computer go into the computer's memory in the form of bytes, and are reflected onto the monitor. These characters are manipulated by the software program you're using. For example, if you're writing a letter to a friend using WordPerfect 5.1, when you save a letter and give it a name, WordPerfect creates a file by copying the characters in RAM to available space on a floppy or hard disk.

The filename and location of the characters in your letter are kept in a place on the disk called the FAT (file allocation table). Any time you want to see the letter again, you tell WordPerfect to get the file by the name you gave it and its characters are copied from the disk it was saved on to the computer RAM so you can work on it. When you decide to print the letter, the characters are sent from computer memory (RAM) through either a serial or parallel port to the printer.

Compatibility

Back when the IBM PC was a new product, many other manufacturers saw the potential in the computer market and developed their own systems. The Tandy Corp. (Radio Shack), like Texas Instruments Inc., thought it could make improvements to the IBM PC and take a larger share of the computer market. This was a mistake because their computers couldn't run IBM-compatible software. Software written for the IBM PC was easy to copy, so many people wanted IBM-compatible machines to avoid having to buy special software. To prove the power of IBM-compatible software, Tandy Inc. is now producing IBM-compatible computers and Texas Instruments Inc., along with many others, have dropped from the personal-computer market.

IBM-compatible computers

No compatible or clone computer is 100% compatible with an IBM computer because the BIOS in the IBM computer has a built-in BASIC routine that will allow only the IBM BASIC programming language to run on an IBM computer. Fortunately, this is a minor problem for owners of IBM-compatible machines because Microsoft DOS, up to version 4.01, comes with GW-BASIC and versions 5.0 and 6.0 come with QBASIC.

From my experience, the most frequent compatibility problems arise from video cards, speed of the bus (slots), and BIOS. Computer systems that are pushed to the limit in speed and video resolution must stray from the conservative standards set by IBM, resulting in possible incompatibility with some software programs.

Avoiding compatibility problems

Like a car, some computers are designed better than others. If you buy the lowest-priced system, you're likely to get components that have compatibility problems or that don't operate with all software programs.

I've found some brand-name systems to have problems because their manufacturers are slow to correct the bugs, and their systems sit in a warehouse becoming outdated.

Computers are so complex that most people don't know what to look for to avoid incompatibility. Your best protection is a guarantee. When you purchase a computer system, ask the salesperson to indicate on your receipt that your system can run the software you want to use. Also, have him write that your system is as compatible as other major systems sold. If you plan to buy an older, used system, you need to be more concerned about compatibility and should test your software on it before you close the deal.

Part two
DOS Training

8 *List of terms*

It's extremely important that you read the following alphabetized list. Knowing these terms will greatly increase your comprehension when reading this book. I'll be referencing these terms throughout the book so you can come back and read what you need, when you need it. If you don't completely understand the definition of the terms as you read them, don't get frustrated because many of them are explained in more detail later in the book.

'286, '386, and '486

These are the names used to describe a computer. They are derived from the type of microprocessor (80286, 80386, or 80486) in that computer.

^Z

The ^Z (Control–Z) character is the end-of-file marker, which you can create by holding down the Ctrl key and hitting the letter Z, or by hitting the F6 function key. When DOS sees the ^Z character in a file, it knows it has found the end of the file. You'll use the ^Z character in chapter 13, *Making a file with COPY CON*.

^C

Create the ^C (Control–C) character by holding down the Ctrl key and hitting the C key. It's used to stop the current operation and return control of the system to the user. For example, you use the DIR command to list the files in a directory of 450 files, rather than wait for the end of the list you can Ctrl–C at any time to stop the DIR command and regain control of the system.

640K bytes The K stands for roughly 1000 bytes, and 640K bytes equals 655,360 bytes. This is the maximum size of base RAM memory. Another name for base memory is *conventional memory*.

ASCII ASCII is the abbreviation for American Standard Code for Information Interchange. For simplicity, consider ASCII characters as the letters, numbers, and symbols on an IBM-compatible keyboard.

AT-compatible computer The IBM AT computer was designed and built by IBM Corporation, and the competition's copy of this computer is called an AT clone or AT-compatible computer. The AT-compatible computer is based on an 80286 microprocessor and is much faster than an XT because it moves 16 bits of data at a time instead of the XT's eight bits.

Backslash The backslash (\) is usually located on the key with the vertical bar or pipe symbol (¦), and is always used to indicate a directory. If, for example, you type in:

```
\NAMES
```

the computer sees a directory. If you type in:

```
NAMES
```

the computer sees a filename.

BIOS BIOS stands for *basic input/output system*. The BIOS program is stored in ROM (Read-only memory) chips, which contain the basic instructions to control the drives, keyboard, and most other input/output operations. The BIOS also boots the computer and loads the DOS system.

Byte A byte is a series of eight bits. Each bit is either an electrical charge or absence of an electrical charge (0 or 1). When grouped in a series, eight bits create one byte. Think of a byte as being equal to one letter or character.

Cache memory Cache memory is a small amount of expensive, very fast memory that's used to hold frequently accessed data from the slower RAM. Retrieving data from cache memory at higher speeds increases processing performance.

CMOS chip A CMOS chip is an integrated circuit usually found in a package called a DIP (direct inline package). CMOS is an abbreviation for Complementary Metal Oxide Semiconductor. Most memory chips are of this type because of their low power usage.

This is the term used to describe turning on the computer or pushing the reset switch. When a computer cold boots, it performs a series of tests and loads the DOS system files from floppy drive A: or hard drive C:.

Cold boot

Commands control and direct the functions of your computer. You can command your computer to format floppy disks, copy files, copy disks, compare files or disks, print documents, and run all the programs on your DOS disk or in your \DOS directory. You can type a DOS command in upper- or lowercase letters, or even a mixture of both. For example:

Commands

```
copy earring.no1 \trinkets
```

is the same as:

```
COPY EARRING.NO1 \TRINKETS
```

is the same as:

```
Copy EARRing.No1 \trinkETS
```

A command statement consists of a DOS command and its related parts (including drive/path designations and switches) that you activate by hitting the Enter or Return key. You can type a command statement in upper- or lowercase or any combination of both. Spaces are used to separate the parts of a command statement. Some examples include:

Command statement

```
DIR
COPY A:\ B:\
BACKUP C:\ A:/s/1
RESTORE A: c:/s
```

When you copy a file, you're making a duplicate file in another directory or on another drive.

Copy

CPU is an abbreviation for *central processing unit* and is the same thing as a microprocessor in a microcomputer. Sometimes the microcomputer without the monitor and keyboard (just the box) is referred to as a CPU. Before the microprocessor was invented, *CPU* referred to the registers, controllers, and ALU (arithmetic logic unit) of a computer.

CPU

This is the directory that DOS is accessing at the present time. After using the *PROMPT PG* command, it's the directory shown at the prompt.

Current directory

The cursor is the blinking figure (usually an underscore) on the monitor. As you type, the cursor moves ahead to indicate where the next character will appear.

Cursor

Defaults Many programs are written to use designated values or parameters if you don't enter any of your own. These values or parameters are called *defaults*. For example, if you type the command DIR, you'll get a listing of the files in the current directory because you didn't specify a drive or directory with the command. The current directory is the default for the DIR command. If you type *DIR \TOYS*, however, you'll get a listing of the files in the \TOYS directory. When you add a directory specification to the DIR command, you indicate that you're not using the default.

Device driver A device driver is a program that, when loaded by the CONFIG.SYS file, becomes part of DOS and enhances its operation.

DEVICEHIGH When using MS-DOS 5.0 or 6.0 in an 80386 or 80486 computer, the DEVICEHIGH command will attempt to load device drivers into the UMA (upper-memory area). This is useful, for example, if you want to load a MOUSE.SYS device driver into the UMA using the CONFIG.SYS file. For examples, see chapter 26, *The CONFIG.SYS file & EDIT* (p. 000).

Directory This is an area on a disk that holds a group of related files to keep them separate from other files.

DOS DOS is the abbreviation for *disk operating system*. DOS is a collection of programs that allow the disk drives, keyboard, and other parts of a computer to communicate and perform special operations. When a computer is turned on, special DOS system files on the hard disk or DOS system disk are automatically loaded into the computer memory. Consider the following idea:

A baby can't walk because it hasn't yet learned how; there's no walking program in the child's brain. In time, with practice, the baby will develop a program and be able to walk. Although a computer doesn't learn, it *does* use a DOS program, which can instruct it to do a specific task. For example, the DOS FORMAT.COM program instructs the floppy drive with the correct sequence of events to produce a formatted floppy disk.

There are three main brands of DOS: IBM DOS, MS-DOS, and DR DOS. PC DOS is another name for IBM DOS. Both IBM DOS and MS-DOS were written by Microsoft, so they're practically identical. Digital Research Corporation produces DR DOS, which is very similar to MS-DOS, and they've just released DR DOS 6.0. MS-DOS and DR DOS commands are very similar, so if you can use one, you should be able to use the other. This book is based on MS-DOS, with a chapter devoted to DR DOS 6.0.

Many MS-DOS versions exist, from 1.0 to 6.0. It's good to have a version of 3.1 or later. Each time changes are made to the current DOS version, it's given a new version number, for example 3.1, 3.2, 3.21, and 3.3. When substantial changes are made, the version jumps a full number, for example

3.0, 4.0, 5.0 and 6.0. A major advancement of MS-DOS 4.0 was the ability to create a hard-drive partition greater than 32 megabytes, which was the maximum partition size of MS-DOS 3.0. The major advancement of MS-DOS 5.0 is the ability to load most of its operating system files and memory-resident programs into extended memory above 1 megabyte, which is called the HMA (high-memory area). MS-DOS 6.0 introduced some new commands, improved the BACKUP command, now called MSBACKUP, and added many new utilities.

When using MS-DOS 5.0 or 6.0, load the DOS=HIGH,UMB command using the CONFIG.SYS file if you want to load the DOS system files into the HMA. For examples see chapter 26, *CONFIG.SYS & EDIT* (p.124).

DOS=HIGH,UMB

This is the main DOS disk, which, when you put it in drive A: and turn on the computer, will give you an A> prompt on the monitor. This disk contains the DOS system files and is labeled *boot disk*, *system disk*, or *master disk*.

DOS system disk

This symbol represents the Enter or Return key. The commands you type using the keyboard aren't acted upon by the computer until you push the Enter key.

Enter

If you have a system with extended memory, you can convert the extended memory to expanded memory by using a software program that tricks the computer into thinking that the extended memory is part of the base memory. For example, if you create a spreadsheet with Lotus 1-2-3 that's too big to fit into base memory, you can run a program to convert your extended memory into expanded memory. Now the spreadsheet will fit because Lotus 1-2-3 uses expanded memory as if it were base memory. Some programs like Windows version 3.*x* and Lotus 1-2-3 version 3.*x* are designed to use extended memory, thereby eliminating the need for expanded memory.

Expanded memory

EMM386.SYS (MS-DOS 4.01) and EMM386.EXE (MS-DOS 5.0 and 6.0) are device drivers, located in the \DOS directory. They're loaded with the CONFIG.SYS file and, with a '386 computer, use extended memory to simulate expanded memory. Also, they're upper-memory-area managers.

Expanded-memory device drivers

Extended memory is RAM that exceeds the 640K base-memory barrier. If you have a computer with 640K RAM, you have no extended memory. If you have a computer with one megabyte of RAM, you have 384K of extended memory.

Extended memory

A file is information that you name and save on a disk. For example, I wrote this list of terms using a word processor and gave it the filename LISTTERM.CHP. A filename consists of a maximum of eight characters on the left side of the period (the filename) and a maximum of three characters

File

8-1
The components of a filename.

from 1 to 8 characters

FILENAME.EXT

from 1 to 3 characters (extension)

on the right side of the period (the extension), as shown in FIG. 8-1. It makes no difference whether you type the filename in upper- or lowercase letters because the computer converts all lowercase letters to uppercase. Examples of filenames are:

AUTOEXEC.BAT	DISKCOPY.COM
M.TXT	CONFIG.SYS
WRITE	533NR&.__$
WORDS.1	$.MON
A	JOHNNY.BOY

The most common file extensions are:

.COM	(executable program)
.EXE	(executable program)
.BAS	(BASIC program)
.BAK	(backup of a text file)
.BIN	(binary file)
.DAT	(data file)
.PAS	(Pascal program)
.SYS	(system file)
.TXT	(text file (ASCII))
.DOC	(data file and also a document file from Microsoft Word)
.TMP	(temporary file)
.DBF	(database file created by dBASE III Plus)
.WK1	(also .WKS created by Lotus 1-2-3)
.BAT	(batch file, for example AUTOEXEC.BAT)
.INI	(initialization file used in Windows programs)

Note: You can't use spaces in a filename. If you need to separate words, use an underscore:

MY_BMW.CAR

A period in a filename can be used only to separate the name and the extension, thus there can be only one period in a filename.

File attribute A file can have any combination of four attributes: read-only, hidden, archive (backed up), or system. Attributes allow you to control files. For example, if you wanted to make sure a file isn't deleted or changed, you can make it read-only.

A 5¼-inch floppy disk is a 5-inch circular plastic disk coated with a magnetic oxide and sealed into a 5¼-inch square plastic protective housing. It's called a floppy because the plastic disk is as thin as a piece of paper and flops when you try to hold it. A 3½-inch floppy disk is a 3⅜-inch magnetic disk housed in a sturdier plastic container, 3½ inches across.

Floppy disk

Formatting is a process in which a disk drive makes a series of magnetized circles on a disk. The magnetized circles are used by the disk drive to locate information. All new disks must be formatted.

Formatting

The forward slash, /, which is on the same key as the question mark, is usually used with DOS commands as a switch. For example, you can use the BACKUP command in several ways. In the following:

Forward slash

```
BACKUP C: A:/s
```

The /s switch means to also back up subdirectories. In this command:

```
BACKUP C: A:/s/m/a/l:
```

the /s switches on subdirectories, /m switches on update, /A means to add to the disk and don't erase it, and /l means create a BACKUP.LOG file so you know what files are on which disk.

The hard drive is a device that contains a fixed nonflexible disk or disks (also called platters) that rotate much faster than a floppy disk. The benefits of the hard-disk drive over the floppy drive are a much higher capacity and much higher data-access speed.

Hard drive

HIMEM.SYS is an extended memory manager that's loaded by the CONFIG.SYS file and is necessary when loading MS-DOS 5.0 or 6.0 system files into the HMA, and TSRs into the UMA. You must have more than one megabyte of RAM to use the HMA. For examples, see chapter 26, *The CONFIG.SYS file & EDIT* (p. 124).

HIMEM.SYS

When using MS-DOS 5.0 or 6.0, HMA is the abbreviation for *high-memory area* and is the first 64K of memory located above 1 megabyte in RAM. MS-DOS 5.0 and 6.0 uses this area in which to load its system files.

HMA

A jumper is usually a metal connector covered with black plastic. It's used to make a connection between two pins on a printed circuit board. Like a switch, if the jumper is on the pins the switch is on, and if the jumper is taken off the pins the switch is turned off.

Jumper

A kilobyte (K) is roughly a thousand bytes. Floppy-drive capacities and smaller-sized RAMs are rated in kilobytes.

Kilobyte

Loadhigh or LH   LOADHIGH is available with MS-DOS 5.0 and 6.0. It's used to load some programs into the UMA after the proper CONFIG.SYS file commands are loaded (HIMEM.SYS, DOS=HIGH,UMB, and EMM386.EXE). For example, to load a mouse-driver program into the UMA, enter the command:

```
LH \MOUSE\MOUSE
```

at the **C>** prompt.

Logical drive   A logical drive is part of the capacity of a physical hard drive (40 megabytes, for example) that's assigned a drive letter (D: through Z:) that acts like it's a separate physical drive.

Math coprocessor   The math coprocessor is a chip that takes over math operations for the microprocessor and can calculate high-level math up to six times faster than the microprocessor. Typical identifying numbers of math coprocessors are 80287-8 and 80387-33. The -8 and -33 at the end of the identifying number is the maximum speed, in Megahertz, at which the coprocessor is rated to operate.

Megabyte   A megabyte (Mb) is roughly a million bytes (1,048,576). Hard-drive capacities and RAM are rated in megabytes.

Microprocessor   The microprocessor is the main computing device, which tells the rest of the system what to do and when to do it. It makes all the decisions and either calculates the math or sends it to the math coprocessor if there's one in the system. Intel Corporation makes most of the microprocessors in IBM-compatible computers, and they're typically designated by the numbers 80286, 80386, and 80486. The most popular microprocessors are:

80386SX-20	(32 bits using 16-bit data access at 20 Megahertz)
80386DX-33	(32 bits using 32-bit data access at 33 Megahertz)
80486SX-25	(486 processor with no math coprocessor, at 25Mhz)
80486DX-50	(486 processor with math coprocessor, at 50Mhz)

Microprocessor speeds are constantly on the rise, so I wouldn't be surprised if the most popular speeds are higher when this book is published.

Network   When two or more computers are connected together so they can share information, you have a network. Usually, one computer is called a file server and its information is accessed by one or more workstations.

Path   A path is the route that a computer follows when it's looking for a DOS program file or executable file. The path command lets you run executable program files located on another drive or in another directory from any drive or directory you're in.

A program is a file with either a .COM or .EXE extension that you can run (execute) by typing its filename and hitting the Enter key. The program file is written in a high-level language and compiled into machine code for fast execution. A program is created to perform a task, such as the FORMAT.COM program (which is used to format disks) or the BACKUP.EXE program (which is used to copy files and directories from your hard drive to floppy disks).

Program

The prompt is composed of the characters on the screen indicating that the computer is waiting for input. Some examples are **C>**, **A>**, and **C:\>**.

Prompt

RAM is the abbreviation for *random-access memory*. RAM is the main memory in your computer. If you type a letter in a word processor, you're entering the information into RAM. If the power goes off, the RAM is reset to zero, and all information that was in the RAM is lost. So remember to save your work frequently to a floppy or hard disk in order to prevent data loss. The most common sizes for RAM are 256K, 512K, and 640K in older computers, and one, two, and four megabytes in newer computers.

RAM

This is the main directory of a floppy or hard disk. The root directory is created when the disk is formatted. All directories and files are contained within the root directory. The root directory for a hard disk, C:, is C:\. For examples, see p.71.

Root directory

When you're using MS-DOS 5.0 or 6.0, use the SETVER command to display and modify the MS-DOS version table; the SETVER.EXE device driver loads the MS-DOS version table into memory. The MS-DOS version table contains a list of programs and the MS-DOS version numbers they're designed to work with. Programs not updated for MS-DOS 5.0 or 6.0 will be fooled into believing they're using the correct MS-DOS version. For examples, see chapter 26, *CONFIG.SYS & EDIT* (p. 124).

SETVER and SETVER.EXE

Shadow RAM is an area of RAM usually located just above the 640K base-memory area (conventional memory). There's a BIOS chip or chips on main computer boards and on color video cards that typically operate at the speed of 200 ns (nanoseconds). RAM typically operates at 80 ns. By copying the BIOS information to RAM at boot up, the computer can read that information from RAM instead of the BIOS chip(s). This will increase the read speed by more than 100%.

Shadow RAM

A subdirectory is a directory within a directory. If you have a directory called \MONEY and you make a directory called \PENNIES in the directory called \MONEY, then the directory \PENNIES is a subdirectory of the directory \MONEY. It's represented as \MONEY\PENNIES.

Subdirectory

System files These are DOS program files that are loaded into memory during the computer boot up. For example, MS-DOS has two hidden system files called MSDOS.SYS and IO.SYS. These two files and COMMAND.COM allow your system to boot up to the **A)** or **C)** prompt.

👁 👁 Note: If for some reason your computer won't boot up from the hard drive, boot it from your DOS system disk and check the root directory of drive C: to make sure that COMMAND.COM is there.

TSR TSRs are programs that reside in a small portion of base (conventional) memory and can be called while a different program is currently running. TSR stands for *terminate and stay resident*; another term is *memory-resident programs*. For example, you could load a calculator as a TSR and then run Lotus 1-2-3. In the middle of creating a spreadsheet you could push the keys Alt–F1 to pop up the calculator and calculate some numbers. When you're finished, you would push the Esc key to clear the calculator and resume work on the spreadsheet.

UMA UMA is the abbreviation for *upper-memory area* and is the 384K of RAM located between conventional (640K) and one megabyte of memory. When using MS-DOS 5.0 or 6.0, you can relocate device drivers and TSRs that would normally be in conventional memory into the UMA, thereby freeing conventional memory for other programs to use.

Wait states Wait states are pauses during CPU processing that allow memory chips enough time to keep up with a microprocessor that accesses them faster than their rated speed.

Warm boot A warm boot occurs when you hold down the Ctrl and Alt keys and push the Del key. The computer performs a quick memory test that doesn't appear on the monitor as it does during a cold boot. You'll want to cold or warm boot your computer if you get stuck or if it freezes or locks up. When you reboot the computer, the RAM is cleared. This process is like wiping the slate clean and starting over again. Try a warm boot first and, if that doesn't work, then hit the good old reset button for a cold boot. If your computer doesn't have a reset button, turn the power switch off for a minute and then back on.

Wildcard The most common wildcard is an asterisk. It can take the place of all eight characters on the left side of the period in a filename and/or all three characters on the right side of the period. *.* is frequently used to copy all files in a directory to another drive or directory.

XT-compatible computer The IBM XT computer was designed and built by IBM Corporation, and a competitor's copy of this computer is called an XT clone or compatible. The XT compatible uses an 8088 microprocessor.

9 The DOS directory

Before going any further, there are two things you should do. The very first thing, if you haven't already, is to read the previous chapter, *List of terms*, which will increase your comprehension level for the following chapters. Secondly, you need to determine if your computer has been DOS formatted and contains a DOS directory.

A DOS directory is an area on your hard drive that contains the program files that are part of the disk operating system (DOS).

What is a DOS directory?

- Type the information that has a gray screen behind it.
- The first floppy drive in your computer is drive A:.
- If you have two floppy drives, the second is drive B:.
- The hard drive (hard disk) in your computer is drive C:.
- The cursor is the blinking light waiting for you to type (p. 14).
- A DOS system disk will boot the computer (p. 39).
- All new disks must be formatted (p. 41).
- DOS version numbers increase as new versions are released (p. 38).
- A directory is an area of a disk that separates related files.

What you should already know

To install DOS on your computer's hard drive, you must create a DOS partition and format the drive so that it boots the computer. Then you have to

DOS installation

create a DOS directory and copy the DOS program files into it. Appendix A gives detailed instructions about partitioning and formatting a hard drive.

Looking for DOS

Let's determine if your computer has been DOS formatted and whether or not it contains a DOS directory. To do this, turn on your computer. If it boots up to a **C>** prompt, the hard drive has been DOS formatted. If it doesn't boot, go to Appendix A, Loading DOS; otherwise, at the **C>** prompt, type:

```
CD\
```

press Enter, and then type:

```
DIR /p
```

and press the Enter key. You'll see something like the following:

```
Volume in drive C has no label
Directory of  C:\
COMMAND  COM        # of bytes   date time
CONFIG   SYS        41
AUTOEXEC BAT        45
DOS           <DIR>
DOS33         <DIR>
DOS5          <DIR>
DRDOS         <DIR>
              xx File(s)       xxxxxx bytes free
```

In this listing, you'll notice four DOS directories, each with a different name. Your DOS directory might have a name like one in the listing. The most widely used and accepted name is DOS, and is typically what you'll have if you buy a new computer. If you have a DOS directory with a name other than DOS, just substitute that name when this book refers to the DOS directory.

Example #1

If you have a DOS directory named DOS5, you want to substitute the following:

```
PATH=C:\DOS5
```

for each instance of the command PATH=C:\DOS.

Example #2

You just bought a used computer and you have two DOS directories: DOS and DOS33. You don't know which directory contains the working version of DOS. What now?

The VER command will print, on the monitor, the current version of DOS (the version booted by the hard drive). At the **C:\DOS>** prompt, type:

```
VER
```

and press the Enter key, and you'll see the following information on the screen:

```
MS-DOS version 3.30
```

Now you know that the hard drive was formatted with DOS version 3.3 and that the DOS33 directory is the correct one to use. If you come to the instruction in this book: *Type PATH=C:\DOS* and press *Enter*, you would type:

```
PATH=C:\DOS33
```

and hit the Enter key instead. Check appendix A if your computer doesn't respond correctly.

10 *Changing disk drives*

You can use the disk drives in your computer (both floppy and hard) to store both data and program files. There are times when you'll want to move from drive to drive to make file manipulation safer and easier.

Why change disk drives?

You should change from one disk drive to another to reduce the amount of typing you need to do. The operations of many DOS commands default to the current drive and directory so you don't need to type the drive letter and path each time you execute a command. You might need to log onto a network by changing to a network drive. It's safer to change to the drive from which you'll be deleting files; you'll learn more about this in chapter 15, *DELETE & UNDELETE*.

What you should already know

- The first floppy drive in your computer is drive A:.
- If you have two floppy drives, the second is drive B:.
- The hard drive (hard disk) in your computer is drive C:.
- The cursor is the blinking light waiting for you to type (p. 14).
- The **C>** or **C:\>** is called the prompt (p. 43).
- Typing PROMPT PG lets you see the current directory, and will change the **C>** to **C:\>** (p. 55).
- A default is a value that's determined by the program and used only if you don't enter your own value (p. 38).

Changing drives is really quite simple. Begin by turning on your computer so you have the **C>** prompt. Insert a floppy disk in each floppy drive in your system and push down the lever(s). Use floppy disks you know have been formatted or that have software programs on them. Brand new disks aren't formatted; if you try to use them before they're formatted you'll get an error message. This message is (for DOS 3.3):

Changing drives

```
Not ready error reading drive A
Abort, Retry, Ignore?
```

and (DOS 5.01, 5.0, and 6.0):

```
Not ready reading drive A (DOS 4.01, 5.0, and 6.0)
Abort, Retry, Fail?
```

If you see this error message, you might have one of the following problems:

- The door on the floppy drive isn't closed.
- The floppy disk wasn't formatted or is faulty.

The following steps will get you back to drive C:. When using DOS 3.*x*, hit the letter A to Abort. You'll get the same message again. Now hit the letter I key for Ignore and you'll see the line:

```
Current drive is no longer valid
```

Now type C: and hit the Enter key, and you'll end up at the **C>** prompt. When using DOS 4.01, 5.0, and 6.0, hit the F key, for Fail, and you'll see the line:

```
Current drive is no longer valid
```

Now type C: and press Enter, and you'll end up at the **C>** prompt.

Don't worry if you get this error message. It's a very common error and everyone using a computer gets it occasionally. Remember, if you have a problem getting back to the C: drive, you can always press the reset button to reboot the computer.

With floppies in drives A: and B:, do the following:

1. Type A: and Enter at the **C>** prompt. This will move you to drive A:.
2. At the **A>** prompt, type C: and Enter. This will move you to drive C:.
3. At the **C>** prompt, type A: and Enter. This will move you back to drive A:.
4. At the **A>** prompt, type B: and Enter (only if you have two floppy drives).

If you type B: and press Enter, and don't have a second floppy drive, you'll get the following message:

```
Insert diskette for drive B: and press any key when ready
```

Hit the Enter key and you'll get a **B>** prompt; Now drive A: will work as if it were drive B:. If you type A: at the **B>** prompt and Enter, you'll get the following message:

```
Insert diskette for drive A: and press any key when ready
```

Hit the Enter key again and you'll be back to the **A)** prompt. This process is useful for copying a file on one floppy disk to another floppy disk, and will be explained in greater detail in chapter 19, *Copying & moving files*. Remember to specify the drive you want by its letter followed by a colon (see FIG. 10-1).

```
A:    B:    C:
|     |     |_____ The hard disk
|     |_____ The second floppy drive
|_____ The first floppy drive
```

10-1
Drive letters and their associated disk drives.

Logical and network drive letters

It's important to know about logical and network drive letters because you might encounter them if you use computers where you work or when installing some types of software.

Logical drive letters

Hard drives are divided into partitions. The first, or *primary*, partition is typically drive C: and, depending upon which version of DOS you use to create it, can be any size, up to the full capacity of the hard drive.

Usually, for organizational purposes, large-capacity hard drives are divided into logical drives. A logical drive is a portion of a hard drive that's assigned a letter and acts as a separate physical hard drive. For example, a 200-megabyte hard drive can be divided into a 100Mb primary partition and a 100Mb secondary partition. The primary partition would be designated the letter C:, and the secondary partition would be designated the logical drive letter D:. Or you could divide the hard disk into multiple partitions and assign them multiple drive letters, up to the letter Z:. Logical drives function just like physical drives.

Network drive letters

Most small networks assign unused logical drive letters to drives of other network computers as a method of accessing those computers' hard drives. The most popular large network software in use is Novell, and it takes control of the drive letters F: through Z:. If you wanted to log onto a Novell network, you would type the letter F: and Enter, and then follow the logon procedure.

Extra practice

To review:

- The standard floppy drives are A: (floppy #1) and B: (floppy #2).
- The hard-disk drive (or fixed disk) is drive C:.
- Logical drive letters begin at D: and end at Z:.
- Logical drives act just like physical drives.
- A Novell network controls the logical drive letters F: through Z:.
- To change from one drive to another, simply type the drive letter followed by a colon, and press the Enter key.
- The PROMPT PG command will show the current directory in the prompt.

At the **C)** prompt, type A: and press Enter to change to the A: drive. Now, at the **A)** prompt, type C: and press Enter to change back to the C: drive. Keep changing to different drive letters until you feel comfortable doing it.

11 DIR

The DIR command is one of the most commonly used commands. It's valuable for locating files and making sure you're in the right directory when copying or deleting groups of files.

The DIR command is used to display the names of the files in a directory. You can add any combination of drive letter, directory names, or file specifications to the DIR command to list the contents of selected parts of a drive. Using the DIR command alone will list all files in the current directory.

Why use DIR?

- Type the information that has a gray screen behide it.
- The first floppy drive is A: and the hard-disk drive is C:.
- The blinking light (usually an underscore) on the monitor is called the cursor (p. 14).
- The **C>** or **C:\>** is called the prompt (p. 43).
- Typing PROMPT PG will enable you to see the current directory in the prompt (p. 55).
- A forward slash (/) is used as a switch to activate alternate parameters available with a command (p. 41).
- All disks that are formatted using DOS (both hard and floppy) will have a root directory (p. 43).
- A file attribute determines if a file is read-only, hidden, archived (backed up), or system (p. 40).

What you should already know

The command DIR *directory switches*

Displaying the directory in the prompt

Usually, when you boot the computer or change to another drive, the computer puts you in the root directory. To be sure you're in the root directory, use the PROMPT command to display the current directory in the prompt. At the **C>** prompt, type:

```
PROMPT $P$G
```

and press Enter. Your **C>** prompt should now look like this:

```
C:\>
```

The backslash means you're in the root directory.

Using the DIR command

Try entering the command D I R at the **C:\>** prompt, and hit the Enter key. You'll see the following:

```
Volume in drive C has no label
Directory of C:\
```

followed by a listing of all the files and directories you have the root C: drive, and the amount of bytes free. Using the DIR command lets you know where your files and directories are located. Now, go to drive A: (you must have a floppy disk in drive A:) and type A: and Enter. Type D I R and Enter, and you'll get a list of the files in the root directory of the floppy disk in drive A:. Now go back to drive C: by typing C: and Enter. Check the root directory of drive C again by typing D I R and pressing Enter.

You can also list the files on any drive or in any other directory without regard to the current drive or directory. Right now the current directory is the root directory of drive C:, which is shown in the prompt. You can list the files in the \DOS directory by typing at the **C:\>** prompt:

```
DIR \DOS
```

and pressing Enter. You'll get the listing you requested, but it will fly by more quickly than you can read it because the \DOS directory contains more than 25 files. If you haven't taken a speed-reading course, DOS has a solution for you.

Using switches

Adding the /p switch will cause the DIR command to scroll the file listing one page at a time. A normal monitor screen page is 25 lines. You'll see the phrase *Press any key to continue . . .* at the bottom of the monitor until the listing is completed. Simply hit a key each time you want to see more of the listing. List the files in the \DOS directory using the /p switch by typing:

```
DIR \DOS /p
```

and pressing Enter. You can also use the /w switch to create a wide listing of a directory. Type:

```
DIR \DOS /w
```

and press the Enter key. As you can see, the files are listed in five columns, so many more files can be listed on one page.

Note: MS-DOS 5.0 and 6.0 shows directories in brackets in a wide listing.

When using MS-DOS 5.0 or 6.0, you can use the /a (attribute) switch, which allows you to list files and directories that meet certain requirements. To list only hidden files, type:

```
DIR /ah
```

and press Enter. You'll see the files IO.SYS and MSDOS.SYS. To list only system files, type:

```
DIR /as
```

and press Enter. You'll see the same files as those listing with the /ah switch, because the two files are both system and hidden files. To list only directories, type:

```
DIR /ad
```

and press Enter. The list you'll see will be directories, not filenames (there aren't any extensions), followed by the designation <DIR>. To list only files (no directories), type:

```
DIR /a-d
```

and press Enter. Note that using the minus sign before the d (-d) causes the opposite of the /d switch, which is not to list directories. This is true when using the minus sign for the other attributes as well. For example, to list files that aren't read-only, type:

```
DIR /a-r
```

and press the Enter key. To list files that are either new or changed since your last backup, type:

```
DIR /aa
```

and press Enter.

You've learned a little about the PROMPT command in this chapter. The next chapter goes into more detail about the PROMPT command and shows you a unique way to use it.

Summary

12 PROMPT

You've had some exposure to the PROMPT command in previous chapters because it was necessary for you to see the current directory in the **A>** or **C>** prompt. This chapter will explain the PROMPT command in more detail.

What does it do?

The PROMPT command enables you to see which directory you're in by adding the name of the directory to the **C>** prompt. You can also add your own message to the prompt.

What you should already know

- Type the information that has a gray screen behind it.
- All files and directories originate from the root directory (p. 43).
- A command is an order you give the computer to make it do something (p. 37).
- A directory is an area of a disk that separates groups of related files from unrelated files (p. 38).
- The current directory is the directory you see in the prompt—in other words, the directory you're in.

The command PROMPT

In the PROMPT PG command, $P stands for the current directory, and $G stands for the **⟩** character.

Turn on your computer so you have a **C⟩** prompt. You know you're in drive C:, but you have no way of knowing which directory you're in (the current directory). Type:

```
PROMPT $P$G
```

and press Enter. In the resulting **C⟩** prompt, you'll see a backslash (\), which, when by itself, designates that you're in the root directory. The directory you're in when you see this prompt:

```
C:\NAMES>
```

is the \NAMES directory. The current directory in the following prompt:

```
C:\PEOPLE>
```

is the \PEOPLE directory. What would happen if you typed only the word PROMPT? Try it. Type:

```
PROMPT
```

and press Enter at the **C:\⟩** prompt. You'll get **C⟩**, a prompt that no longer displays the current directory.

Look at the **C⟩** prompt. Which directory are you in? You could be in the \PEOPLE directory or the \NAMES directory or any directory on the disk. There's no way you can know exactly which directory you're in from looking at this **C⟩** prompt. Now enter the command:

```
PROMPT $P$G
```

and press Enter, and the prompt will once again display the current directory. Just for fun, try typing:

```
PROMPT Yes Master?$_$P$G
```

and press Enter. You'll see the following:

```
Yes Master?
C:\>
```

Now your computer knows who the master is. When you finish this book, your computer will no doubt be bowing at your feet! To change back to the standard prompt, type:

```
PROMPT $P$G
```

and press the Enter key.

Summary

In chapter 25, you'll learn how to make an AUTOEXEC.BAT file that will automatically load the PROMPT command each time you turn on the computer. Don't you just love computers? Yeah!

13 Making a file with copy con

Files are the lifeblood of a computer system. Files store data and control the operation of the computer system by carrying bytes (characters) to and from different parts of the system.

Before you start the exercises in this chapter, you want to see the current directory in the prompt, so type the following command:

```
PROMPT $P$G
```

at the **C>** prompt. The backslash (\) in the resulting prompt means that the root directory is current.

What is a file?

A file is information you save onto a hard or floppy drive. A file could be a document created with a word processor or a mailing list created with a database program. When you create a file, the computer records the name of the file (its filename) and the disk location of the bytes in the file in the file-allocation table (FAT). There are three main types of files (illustrated in FIG. 13-1):

ASCII files   These contain only the characters you can type with the keyboard. You'll be making some ASCII files later in this chapter to use throughout the book.

Data files   These contain the characters from the keyboard and also control codes and graphics characters that are created by word processors and similar application programs.

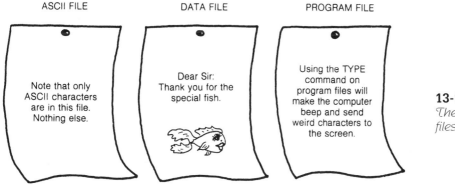

ASCII FILE

Note that only ASCII characters are in this file. Nothing else.

DATA FILE

Dear Sir: Thank you for the special fish.

PROGRAM FILE

Using the TYPE command on program files will make the computer beep and send weird characters to the screen.

13-1
The three basic types of files.

Program files   These are created by compiling files written by programming languages like C, Cobol, and BASIC. Compiling converts the file written by the programming language into machine language so it runs faster. Because program files are compiled, you can't use the DOS TYPE command to read the contents of these files. Program files are frequently executable files, so have an .EXE or .COM extension. WP.EXE and FORMAT.COM are examples of program files.

What you should already know

- Type the information that has a gray screen behide it.
- Pushing the F6 function key gives you the character ^Z (p. 35).
- A command is an order you give the computer to make it do something (p. 37).
- A command statement is a phrase consisting of a command and its related parts (p. 37).
- The prompt will show the current directory when you type PROMPT PG (p. 55).
- Typing PATH C:\DOS will let you use DOS commands from anywhere in the computer (p. 89).
- The root directory is the area on a disk that contains all other files and directories (p. 43).
- A filename consists of a maximum of eight characters to the left of the period and a maximum of three characters to the right of the period (the extension). Example filenames are AUTOEXEC.BAT and BIRD.1 (p. 39).
- A filename and extension can never contain spaces.

The command

COPY CON *filename*

Making ASCII files with COPY CON

You can use COPY CON to make an ASCII text file that will store information or perform multiple operations, such as automatically changing system parameters and executing commands when you boot your system. The command COPY CON means to copy from the console (or keyboard). Near the end of this book, you'll use the COPY CON command to make CONFIG.SYS and AUTOEXEC.BAT files, which will configure your system and execute multiple commands. The files you make in this section will simply store information.

  Note: If you make a mistake, hold down the Ctrl key and hit the letter C to cancel making a file. Then retype the COPY CON command statement to start over again. Practice makes perfect. Make a file with the name BOB.TXT by entering the following lines, following each one with an Enter (and push the F6 function key to get the ^Z to end the file):

```
COPY CON BOB.TXT
My name is Bob.
The end of this file.
^Z
```

Figure 13-2 explains what the different parts of the command COPY CON BOB.TXT mean.

13-2
A description of the parts of a basic command statement.

Use the DIR command to be sure BOB.TXT was created. The directory you generate should list the file BOB.TXT, containing 41 bytes of data. Now make three more files with the names JOHN.DOC, SUE.GRL, and MARY.GRL, using the same procedure you used with BOB.TXT:

```
COPY CON JOHN.DOC
This is John's file.
The end of this file.
^Z
```

```
COPY CON SUE.GRL
My name is Sue.
End of file.
^Z
```

```
COPY CON MARY.GRL
Hello, my name is Mary.
The end.
^Z
```

You've just created four ASCII text files. Try making a file using your name for the filename:

```
COPY CON Richard
Hello, my name is Richard.
You should know how to use the COPY CON command.
This is an ASCII file. It contains only text.
^Z
```

Now use the DIR command to be sure you created all these files correctly:

```
BOB        TXT    41
JOHN       DOC    45
SUE        GRL    31
MARY       GRL    35
Richard           123
```

And you thought this would be difficult!

Summary

You just made a number of ASCII text files. You can view the text you typed into those files on the monitor using the TYPE command, which is covered in the next chapter.

14 TYPE

DOS gives you the TYPE command so you can view the contents of an ASCII file. You can use the MORE filter with the TYPE command to show one screen of data at a time. A *filter* alters the output of a command.

Why type a file?

Some ASCII files store data, and others execute a series of commands and set parameters.

The AUTOEXEC.BAT and CONFIG.SYS files are ASCII files that contain a list of command statements. You can display these files on the monitor using the TYPE command. Some software programs use ASCII files to store data. The communication program ProComm (shareware version) comes with an instruction manual contained in an ASCII file that you can TYPE to either the monitor or printer. Many software programs have files with the names READ.ME or README, which contain data about the program. You can TYPE the contents of these files to the monitor or printer.

As shown in FIG. 14-1, you don't need to specify that data output is to be displayed on the monitor. The TYPE command knows to send all output to the monitor without being told to do so. This is called *defaulting to the monitor*.

14-1
A command statement showing how to type a file.

- Enter means to press the Enter key.
- ASCII files typically contain the characters you see on the keyboard (p. 56).
- Data files can contain graphics and control characters (p. 56).
- Program files are compiled and not legible when using the TYPE command (p. 57).
- You can use the COPY CON command to create an ASCII file (p. 58).
- Pushing the F6 function key gives you the character ^Z (p. 35).

What you should already know

```
TYPE filename parameters
```

The command

TYPE the contents of the BOB.TXT file you created in the last chapter by typing TYPE BOB.TXT and Enter. You'll see the following on your monitor:

```
My name is Bob.
The end of this file.
```

Using the TYPE command

Now look at the other ASCII files you created. Type TYPE MARY.GRL and Enter, and you'll see:

```
Hello, my name is Mary.
The end.
```

Type TYPE SUE.GRL and Enter, and you'll see:

```
My name is Sue.
End of file.
```

Finally, type TYPE JOHN.DOC and Enter, and you'll see:

```
This is John's file.
The end of this file.
```

As you now know, using the TYPE command by itself will send the contents of a file to the monitor. If you want to send a file to the printer connected to your computer, simply add >PRN to the command statement.

Printing a file with TYPE

If you have a printer, be sure it's on line (ready to accept data) and has paper inserted. If you don't have a printer, skip the following exercise.

To TYPE a file to a printer instead of the monitor, type TYPE BOB.TXT >PRN and press Enter. You just sent the file data to the printer instead of the screen. Try it now without the >PRN and see what happens. Type TYPE BOB.TXT and press Enter. The file will go to the monitor as before.

Let's send the contents of another ASCII file to the printer. Type TYPE MARY.GRL >PRN and Enter. The file MARY.GRL will be printed.

You can use the >PRN specification to send other information, like a file listing (directory) to your printer. Issue the command DIR >PRN and Enter. Now you have a printed list of your root directory, which should include the following files:

```
BOB     TXT    41
JOHN    DOC    45
SUE     GRL    31
MARY    GRL    35
```

The MORE filter You can use the MORE filter with the TYPE command to display a long file, one screen at a time. — More —, located at the bottom of the screen, indicates that there's more of the file to be displayed. Hit any key when you want to see it.

Let's make a file 30 lines in length. At the **C:\>** prompt, type COPY CON TEST.TMP and press Enter, and then enter the following lines (make sure to put an Enter after each one:

```
LINE 1
2
3
4
5
6
7
8
9
10
11
12
13
14
15
16
17
18
19
20
21
22
LINE 23
24
25
26
27
28
29
```

```
30 end of file
^Z
```

Now let's TYPE the TEST.TMP file with the command TYPE TEST.TMP and press Enter. You'll see the following on your screen:

```
8
9
10
11
12
13
14
15
16
17
18
19
20
21
22
LINE 23
24
25
26
27
28
29
30 end of file
```

As you can see, the beginning of the file has scrolled by, leaving only lines 8 through 30. Now try the TYPE command with the MORE filter. Type TYPE TEST.TMP ¦ MORE and Enter. (Note: you have to precede MORE with the vertical bar, or pipe, symbol.) You'll see the following:

```
LINE 1
2
3
4
5
6
7
8
9
10
11
12
13
14
15
16
17
```

```
18
19
20
21
22
LINE 23
-- more --
```

Using the MORE filter enables you to see a file, one screen at a time. Simply hit a key to see the rest of the file:

```
10
11
12
13
14
15
16
17
18
19
20
21
22
LINE 23
-- more --
24
25
26
27
28
29
30 end of file
```

Note: A portion of the previous screen is redisplayed in this example because your second screen of information is less than an entire page long.

Summary

Now you can access data in an ASCII file and send it to the printer. You can also use the MORE filter to modify the output of the TYPE command so you can read a long ASCII file one screen at a time.

15 DELETE & UNDELETE

If you couldn't delete files from your computer system, they would pile up until finding a file would be like looking for a needle in a haystack. Delete a file when you no longer need it, or if you need to make room for other files on either a floppy or hard disk.

- Enter means to press the Enter key.
- A filename consists of between one and eight characters on the left side of the period and a file extension of from zero to three characters on the right side of the period (p. 39).
- The TYPE command enables you to list the contents of a text file (p. 60).
- The COPY CON command means *copy from the console* (p. 58).
- Pushing the F6 function key gives you the character ^Z (p. 35).

What you should already know

```
DEL filename
UNDELETE filename
```

The commands

First, make a file so you have something to delete. Make sure you're in your C: root directory (**C:\>**) and type:

Using the DEL command

```
COPY CON OLDSHOES.TMP
This is a temporary file
which will be deleted.
^Z
```

This is so much fun, let's make a couple more files (remember to hit Enter after each line and press the F6 key for the ^Z):

```
COPY CON DIRTYSOX.TMP
Dirtysox.tmp is also a
temporary file.
^Z

COPY CON CRAZYBUG.TMP
A temporary file of bugs
^Z
```

Now you have three files to delete. These files have a .TMP extension to denote that they're temporary files, but remember that you can delete any file with any name and extension.

It's time to check the root directory for our new files! At the **C:\>** prompt, type DIR and Enter. You should see the following:

```
BOB        TXT   41
JOHN       DOC   45
SUE        GRL   31
MARY       GRL   35
OLDSHOES   TMP   50
DIRTYSOX   TMP   42
CRAZYBUG   TMP   27
```

listed along with the rest of the files in your root directory.

Now let's get rid of the OLDSHOES.TMP file. At the **C:\>** prompt, type:

```
DEL OLDSHOES.TMP
```

and press Enter. The only way you can be sure the file was deleted is by using the DIR command.

Now say goodbye to DIRTYSOX.TMP and CRAZYBUG.TMP by typing:

```
DEL DIRTYSOX.TMP
```

and Enter, and then:

```
DEL CRAZYBUG.TMP
```

and Enter. Again, typing DIR and pressing Enter at the **C:\>** prompt should show that these files no longer exist. You should see the following files:

```
BOB    TXT   41
JOHN   DOC   45
SUE    GRL   31
MARY   GRL   35
```

Nice job! You now know how to delete files.

UNDELETE is available only in MS-DOS 5.0 and 6.0. If you accidentally delete the wrong file or group of files, you can recover them with the UNDELETE command.

Filenames are stored in an area on a disk called the file-allocation table (FAT). When a file is deleted, DOS doesn't erase it from the disk. It simply replaces the first letter of the filename with a ? character. When you add a file to the disk that contains the deleted file, DOS first looks in the FAT for filenames with a ? as the first character and writes the new files to that space. For this reason, if you delete a file and decide to undelete it, don't put it off. Undelete the file right away, because the sooner you do it, the better chance that you'll be able to save it.

If you have MS-DOS 5.0 or 6.0 installed on your computer, you can do the following exercise. You'll make a file, delete it, and then undelete it. First, at the **C:** prompt, type:

```
COPY CON TEMP.DOC
```

and Enter. Then use the DEL command to erase the file by typing:

```
DEL TEMP.DOC
```

and Enter.

Use the DIR command to be sure TEMP.DOC is gone, and then use the UNDELETE command to bring it back by typing:

```
UNDELETE C:\TEMP.DOC
```

and Enter. You'll see something like the following:

```
Directory: C:\
File Specifications: TEMP.DOC

     Deletion-tracking file not found.

     MS-DOS directory contains  1 deleted files.
     Of those,  1 files may be recovered.

Using the MS-DOS directory.

     ?EMP    DOC    25 10-23-91 9:39a ...A Undelete (Y/N)?y
     Please type the first character for ?EMP  .DOC:
```

Type the letter T at the prompt, and you'll see the following:

```
File successfully undeleted.
```

Use the DIR command again to see if the TEMP.DOC file is back.

- If you delete a file, don't write to the disk or you probably won't be able to recover the deleted file.
- If you delete a file and then remove the directory it was in, the deleted file won't be recoverable.

- When using MS-DOS 5.0, you can get instant information about the UNDELETE command by using the /? or HELP command. Just type `HELP UNDELETE` and Enter, or `UNDELETE /?` and Enter.
- When using MS-DOS 6.0, you can get instant information about the UNDELETE command by using the /? or FASTHELP command. Type either `FASTHELP UNDELETE` and Enter, or `UNDELETE /?` and Enter. You can get more detailed help by typing `HELP UNDELETE` and Enter.

16 Making directories

Being able to make directories is so important that I've included many examples and practice sessions. Understanding the directory concept isn't the easiest thing to do, so to prevent you from getting frustrated I've included some illustrations in this chapter.

A directory is an area of a hard or floppy disk that has a name and contains related files that are separate from other files in the root directory. Every disk has a root directory, which is created by DOS. All directories you create are contained in the root directory. Although directories created in the root directory are subdirectories of the root directory, they are referred to as *directories*. A *subdirectory* is a directory that is contained in any directory other than the root directory.

What is a directory?

The root directory is created when you format the disk using DOS. Assuming the hard disk in FIG. 16-1 is a 20-megabyte disk, the root directory would have a capacity of 20Mb. The number of free megabytes in the root directory will decrease in proportion to the number of megabytes consumed by files copied to the hard disk.

In FIG. 16-1, try to visualize the \NAMES directory expanding into the free disk space as more and more files are added to the \NAMES directory. Also, if you add files to the \CARS directory, it will expand into the free disk space.

16-1
A hard disk (platter) from inside a hard drive.

HARD DISK

ROOT DIRECTORY

JIM
SUE
SAM
BOB
PAM
JOHN

Free Disk Space

\NAMES

\CARS

Directories inside the ROOT directory

In FIG. 16-2, you can see how the root directory is the starting point for all other directories and subdirectories. The items in the first column to the right of the root directory, starting with \DOS, are considered directories because they branch directly off the root directory. All other directories, in further right columns, are subdirectories of a particular directory.

Figure 16-3 will help you understand how the hard-disk space is occupied with data. The glass on the left shows an empty root directory with a capacity of 20Mb. The glass in the center shows a \DOS directory containing 1Mb of files, leaving 19Mb of free space. The glass on the right contains two directories, \DOS and \LOTUS123. Now what happens if you add 1Mb of files to the \DOS directory in this glass? The \DOS directory would expand to accept the new files using 1Mb of the 17Mb of free disk space.
Figure 16-4 shows the directory structure of a disk. The entire book shelf is the root directory. The loose files on the top shelf are in the root directory because they aren't contained in any other directory. There are also four directories inside the root directory: \NAMES, \PEOPLE, \BOOKS, and \TOYS. These four directories also contain files like the loose ones on the top shelf. A good directory structure can organize your hard disk the way a file cabinet can organize papers and documents.

The grocery store in FIG. 16-5 is like a root directory because it contains all types of food, just like the root directory contains all types of files. Putting all your files in the root directory would be like throwing all the food in the

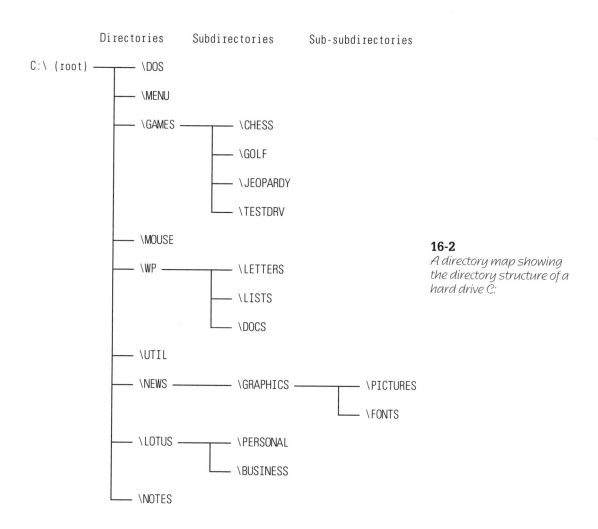

Directories	Subdirectories	Sub-subdirectories

```
C:\ (root) ── ┬── \DOS
              ├── \MENU
              ├── \GAMES ──── ┬── \CHESS
              │               ├── \GOLF
              │               ├── \JEOPARDY
              │               └── \TESTDRV
              ├── \MOUSE
              ├── \WP ──────── ┬── \LETTERS
              │               ├── \LISTS
              │               └── \DOCS
              ├── \UTIL
              ├── \NEWS ─────── \GRAPHICS ──── ┬── \PICTURES
              │                                └── \FONTS
              ├── \LOTUS ───── ┬── \PERSONAL
              │               └── \BUSINESS
              └── \NOTES
```

16-2
A directory map showing the directory structure of a hard drive C:

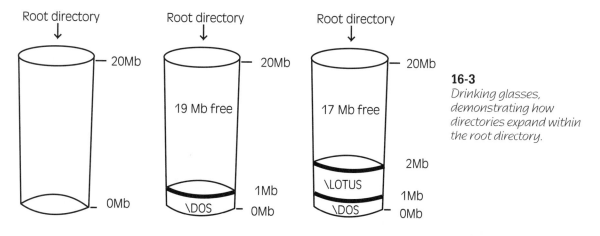

16-3
Drinking glasses, demonstrating how directories expand within the root directory.

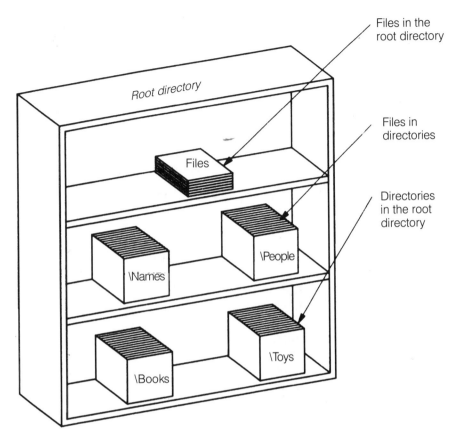

16-4 *A bookcase, illustrating files and directories in the root directory.*

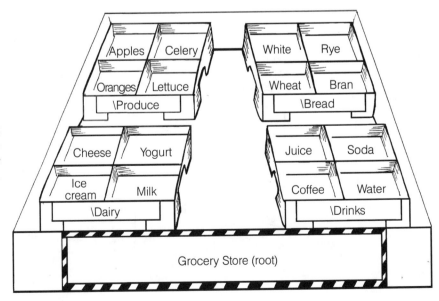

16-5
A grocery store, giving an everyday example of the directory structure.

grocery store on the floor. If you wanted to find an orange, you would have to dig through all the other food until you found it. The counters in the grocery store are like the directories in the root directory. They keep every related item together and separated from other unrelated items.

- Enter means to press the Enter key.
- When you COPY a file, you make a duplicate (p. 37).
- Use the backslash character (\) to specify a directory (p. 36).
- The backslash key is usually located on the key with the vertical bar, or pipe symbol (¦).
- The forward slash, / (located on the ? key), is never used to indicate a directory; it is used to specify command switches, or parameters (p. 41).

What you should already know

```
MD \directoryname
```

The command

First, make a directory called \NAMES by typing, at the **C:\>** prompt, MD \NAMES and Enter.

Making directories

Note: If you get the error message *Unable to create directory*, it's probably because a directory with the same name already exists, or you made a typing error. Try retyping the command. Use the DIR command to check for the \NAMES directory. In addition to the other files in your root directory, you should see NAMES. You can tell it's a directory and not a file because it's followed by the designation <DIR>.

Use the DIR command to check for the directory by typing DIR at the **C:\>** prompt. You should see the following:

```
NAMES    <DIR>
```

added to the files you already have on your root directory. Now copy the file BOB.TXT to the \NAMES directory by typing the command:

```
COPY BOB.TXT \NAMES
```

and Enter. Figure 16-6 explains what the different parts of the command statement COPY BOB.TXT \NAMES means. Now, look in the \NAMES directory for the file BOB.TXT by typing the command:

```
DIR \NAMES
```

and Enter. If you've done everything correctly, you should see the following:

```
BOB    TXT    41
```

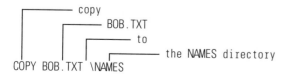

16-6
A command statement, showing the direction for copying a file in to a directory.

```
   3 file(s)   #### bytes free
```

Remember, when the computer sees the backslash (\) in front of the word NAMES, it knows you mean the directory \NAMES. If you forget the backslash and just type NAMES, the computer would assume you meant a file called NAMES and not a directory.

Now copy more files into the \NAMES directory with the following commands (make sure to follow each one with an Enter):

```
COPY JOHN.DOC \NAMES
COPY SUE.GRL \NAMES
COPY MARY.GRL \NAMES
```

Now take another look in the \NAMES directory. Use the DIR command followed by the directory name, like this:

```
DIR \NAMES
```

and Enter. They should all be there, as shown:

```
 Volume in drive C has no label
 Directory of C:\NAMES
.        <DIR>
..       <DIR>
BOB   TXT 41
JOHN  DOC 45
SUE   GRL 31
MARY  GRL 35
   6 file(s)   #### of bytes free
```

Make another directory called \PEOPLE, by typing:

```
MD \PEOPLE
```

and Enter. Use the DIR command to be sure the \PEOPLE directory was created. You should see the entry:

```
PEOPLE   <DIR>
```

It looks like you did it again. Wonderful. Look in the \NAMES directory. At the **C:** type:

```
DIR \NAMES
```

and Enter. Now look in the \PEOPLE directory by typing:

```
DIR \PEOPLE
```

and Enter. As shown:

```
 Volume in drive C has no label
 Directory of C:\PEOPLE
.        <DIR>
..       <DIR>
   2 file(s)   #### bytes free
```

the \PEOPLE directory is empty. The dots represent the directory creation data. All directories and subdirectories have these dots except the root directory.

Now copy the files SUE.GRL and MARY.GRL into the \PEOPLE directory with the following commands (don't forget the Enters!):

```
COPY SUE.GRL \PEOPLE
COPY MARY.GRL \PEOPLE
```

Now look into the \PEOPLE directory by typing DIR \PEOPLE and Enter. You should see the following:

```
 Volume in drive C has no label
 Directory of C:\PEOPLE
.      <DIR>
..     <DIR>
SUE    GRL 31
MARY GRL 35
  4 file(s)    #### of bytes free
```

now have copies of SUE.GRL and MARY.GRL in the root directory, the \PEOPLE directory, and the \NAMES directory.

Remember that the root directory (C:\) is the main directory of any disk. If you get lost in the directory structure, you can always get back to the root directory by typing CD \ and Enter.

Summary

Now that you know how to make directories, you need to know how to change directories. When you change directories, you make another directory the current directory. The next chapter shows you how to change directories.

Changing directories

Moving from one directory to another is easy to do and can save you time and effort when using other commands.

Why change directories?

You change directories when you want to make a different directory the current directory. Usually, it's easier to accomplish certain tasks when you're in the directory with which you're working. Being in a directory also allows you to use commands with their defaults.

What you should already know

- Enter means to press the Enter key.
- A directory is an area on a disk that holds related files (p. 38).
- Use the MD command to make directories (p. 73).
- Use the backslash, \, to indicate a directory (p. 36).
- The `PROMPT $P$G` command shows the current directory in the prompt (p. 55).
- Pushing the F6 function key gives you the character ^Z (p. 35).

The command

`CD\`*directoryname*

Changing directories

Changing directories is when you leave one area of a disk and enter another. The big advantage is that you can use commands without needing to enter the drive letter and path for the current directory. Now, go to the \NAMES directory by typing the following at the **C:\\>** prompt, followed by an Enter:

```
CD \NAMES
```

Note: If you've entered the PROMPT PG command to see the current directory in the prompt, when you change from the root directory to the \NAMES directory, the word NAMES will appear in the **C>** prompt. This indicates that \NAMES is the current directory. The DIR command will show you what is contained in the \NAMES directory:

```
Volume in drive C has no label
Directory of C:\NAMES
.          <DIR>
..         <DIR>
BOB    TXT      41
JOHN   DOC      45
SUE    GRL      31
MARY   GRL      35
    6 file(s)    #### of bytes free
```

Now change back to the root directory with the command CD \ and Enter. The backslash in the resulting prompt indicates that the root directory is now current. Now type in the command DIR and Enter to see what's in the root directory.

Note: When you change to another directory, it's good practice to always use the DIR command to list the contents.

Change back to the \NAMES directory with the command CD \NAMES and Enter. Now change to the \PEOPLE directory without first going back to the root directory by typing the command CD\PEOPLE and Enter. Now the \PEOPLE directory is the current directory. Check to see what's in the \PEOPLE directory with the command DIR and Enter. Now go back to the root directory with CD\ and Enter.

I think it's time to make a couple new directories. Enter the following commands at the **C:\>**, followed by Enters:

```
MD \TOYS
MD \BOOKS
```

Again, type DIR and Enter to verify that these two new directories actually exist. Now, let's change to several directories for the practice:

1. Change to the \BOOKS directory with the command CD \BOOKS and Enter.
2. Change to the \TOYS directory with CD \TOYS and Enter. Now change to the \PEOPLE directory with CD \PEOPLE and Enter.
3. Change to the \NAMES directory with CD \NAMES and Enter.
4. Now change back to the root directory by typing CD \ and Enter.

Remember, the backslash by itself means the root directory. Now, from the root directory, you can see what's in the \TOYS directory. Type the following command:

```
DIR \TOYS
```

followed by an Enter. The \TOYS directory should be empty. Now change to the \TOYS directory with:

```
CD \TOYS
```

and Enter. Now the \TOYS directory is current. List the files in the \TOYS directory with the command DIR and Enter. You can also look at the contents of another directory from the \TOYS directory, with the command:

```
DIR \BOOKS
```

and Enter. You're still in the \TOYS directory, but you've listed the files in the \BOOKS directory. Now change to the \BOOKS directory with:

```
CD \BOOKS
```

and Enter. Because you're in the \BOOKS directory, just type DIR and Enter for a listing of the files in the \BOOKS directory (none, because the directory is empty). Now do a listing of the files in the \NAMES directory with the command DIR \NAMES and Enter.

Put a floppy disk with software on it in drive A, and type DIR A:\ and Enter. You'll see the following:

```
Volume in drive A has no label
Directory of A:\
```

followed by a listing of any files that are on that disk. You've just listed the files on the floppy disk in drive A: without leaving the \BOOKS directory on drive C:.

This is a good time to make a file in the \TOYS directory. Issue the command CD \TOYS and Enter, and then the command COPY CON FIREBIRD.CAR and Enter. Type the following lines into the FIREBIRD.CAR file (don't forget to end each line with an Enter):

```
The firebird is a sports car.
It is fun to drive.
The end.
^Z
```

Look in the \TOYS directory now (DIR \TOYS and Enter) to see what's there. You should see the following:

```
  Volume of drive C has no label
  Directory of C:\TOYS
.            <DIR>
..           <DIR>
FIREBIRD CAR  60
      3 file(s)       #### of bytes free
```

This next step might look complicated, but don't chicken out now. I want you to copy the FIREBIRD.CAR file to the \BOOKS directory. At the **C:\TOYS>** prompt, type, followed by an Enter:

```
COPY FIREBIRD.CAR \BOOKS
```

To verify that you really made a copy in the \BOOKS directory, type the command `DIR \BOOKS` and Enter. You should see the following:

```
Volume of drive C has no label
Directory of C:\BOOKS
.          <DIR>
..         <DIR>
FIREBIRD CAR   60
  3 file(s)      #### of bytes free
```

But wait—something is wrong. The file FIREBIRD.CAR should actually be in a directory \CAR, not in the \TOYS or \BOOKS directory. So let's fix it.

First, make a directory \CARS by typing the command `MD\CARS` and Enter. Now copy the FIREBIRD.CAR file to the \CARS directory with the following command, followed by an Enter:

```
COPY FIREBIRD.CAR \CARS
```

Before you delete the FIREBIRD.CAR file from the \TOYS directory, however, it's a good idea to check the \CARS directory to be sure the FIREBIRD.CAR file was copied. List the files in the \CARS directory with `DIR \CARS` and enter:

```
Volume of drive C has no label
Directory of C:\CARS
.          <DIR>
..         <DIR>
FIREBIRD CAR   60
    3 file(s)      #### of bytes free
```

The FIREBIRD.CAR file is definitely in the \CARS directory, so you can now delete it from the other two directories.

At the **C:\TOYS>** prompt, type the command:

```
DEL FIREBIRD.CAR
```

and Enter. Now look in the \TOYS directory to be sure the FIREBIRD.CAR file is gone, with `DIR` and Enter. It's gone, alright. Now erase the file from the \BOOKS directory by typing:

```
DEL BOOKS\FIREBIRD.CAR
```

and Enter. Check the directory by typing:

```
DIR \BOOKS
```

and Enter. This is easier than you thought. Right?

Practice makes perfect, so here it is:

```
CD \
CD \PEOPLE
CD \BOOKS
CD \NAMES
CD \CARS
CD \
DIR
```

18 Removing directories

There are times when you'll have empty directories because you deleted files to make more disk space available. You should remove those empty directories and subdirectories.

Why remove a directory?

If you don't remove your unused directories, it will be more difficult to find the directories and files you want when using the DIR command. Remove directories that are no longer useful to maintain an efficient system. Removing empty directories also makes more disk space available.

What you should already know

- Enter means pressing the Enter key.
- The command MD stands for *make directory* (p. 73).
- The command CD means *change directory* (p. 76).
- The backslash key (\) is used to indicate a directory (p. 36).
- A subdirectory is a directory inside a directory (p. 43).

The command

RD *filename*

First, make a directory called \BOATS with the command:

```
MD \BOATS
```

Making & removing directories

and Enter (at the **C:** prompt). Now remove the directory \BOATS with:

```
RD \BOATS
```

and Enter. Make a directory called \TREE by typing:

```
MD \TREE
```

and Enter, and then remove the \TREE directory with:

```
RD \TREE
```

and Enter. Make a directory called \BIRDS with:

```
MD \BIRDS
```

and Enter, and remove it with:

```
RD \BIRDS
```

and Enter. Now try to remove the \NAMES directory (RD \NAMES and Enter) and see what happens. You'll see the following on your screen:

```
Invalid path, not directory,
or directory not empty
```

If you get this message, it's because the directory you're trying to remove has a file or a subdirectory in it. You have to delete all the files and subdirectories from the directory you want to remove.

Note: If you try to remove an empty directory and still get an error message, it's likely that there are hidden files in the directory that won't show up with the DIR command (unless you use the MS-DOS 5.0 or 6.0 command DIR /ah). You won't be able to remove that directory no matter what you do until you delete those files. Don't worry about it now. I'm just telling you about it so you don't go crazy wondering why you can't remove a particular directory.

Making & removing sub-directories

Issue the following commands from the **C:** prompt, following each line with an Enter:

```
MD \VEGGIES
MD \VEGGIES\CARROTS
MD \VEGGIES\CELERY
```

Now look in the \VEGGIES directory by typing:

```
DIR \VEGGIES
```

and Enter. You'll see the following:

```
 Volume of drive C has no label
 Directory of C:\VEGGIES
.          <DIR>
..         <DIR>
CARROTS    <DIR>
CELERY     <DIR>
        4 file(s)      #### of bytes free
```

Now remove all three directories. Try to remove the \VEGGIES directory first, with:

```
RD \VEGGIES
```

and Enter. You'll get the *directory not empty* error message, which occurred because there are two subdirectories in the \VEGGIES directory. You must completely empty the \VEGGIES directory of files and subdirectories before you can remove it. Remove the subdirectories with the commands:

```
RD \VEGGIES\CARROTS
RD \VEGGIES\CELERY
```

Now remove the \VEGGIES directory:

```
RD \VEGGIES
```

(Remember to hit Enter after each line.) You've just removed all three directories and subdirectories.

Note: If you have the prompt C:\VEGGIES>, you can't remove the \VEGGIES directory because it's the current directory. Use the command:

```
CD \
```

and Enter to change to the root directory, and then use the command:

```
RD \VEGGIES
```

and Enter to remove the \VEGGIES directory. Check to be sure the \VEGGIES directory is gone with DIR and Enter. As you can see, there's no more \VEGGIES directory.

Note: MS-DOS 6.0 introduced the new command DELTREE so you can remove a directory and all its files and subdirectories with one command statement. You'll find detailed information and examples in chapter 25, *XCOPY & DELTREE*.

19 Copying & moving files

It's inevitable that you'll need to copy files—even if it's only from your word-processing directory to a floppy disk. Some word-processing programs like WordPerfect let you copy files while in a directory listing. This chapter will teach you how to copy any file to any drive or directory. MS-DOS 6.0 introduced a new command, called MOVE, with which you can relocate a file or group of files. You can also use it to rename a directory.

Before you begin, use the PROMPT command to show the current directory. At the DOS prompt, type PROMPT PG and Enter.

Why copy a file?

You copy when you want to duplicate a file or group of files onto a floppy disk, hard drive, or another directory.

What you should already know

- The COPY CON command means *copy from console* (p. 58).
- ASCII, data, and program are the three basic types of files (p. 56).
- The PROMPT PG command will show the current directory in the prompt (p. 55).
- The asterisk is called a *wildcard*, and is used to take the place of some or all characters in a filename. For example, *.* means all filenames (p. 44).
- The MD command means *make directory* (p. 73).
- The CD command means *change directory* (p. 76).
- The RD command means *remove directory* (p. 81).

The command statement in FIG. 19-1 reads: *COPY the file JOHN.DOC to the \PEOPLE directory*. Studying this statement will help you to remember the proper sequence of file and directory.

```
                copy
              JOHN.DOC
                        to
                            the PEOPLE directory
COPY JOHN.DOC \PEOPLE
```

19-1
A description of the COPY *command.*

Copying files is easy once you become used to the way the command statements are written. Begin by copying the JOHN.DOC file to the \PEOPLE directory. Type `COPY JOHN.DOC \PEOPLE` and Enter. Then use the DIR command to look into the \PEOPLE directory (`DIR \PEOPLE` and Enter):

How to copy files

```
Volume in drive C has no label
Directory of C:\people
.          <DIR>
..         <DIR>
SUE     GRL     31
MARY    GRL     35
JOHN    DOC     45
    5 file(s)        #### of bytes free
```

Now copy BOB.TXT into the \PEOPLE directory, with the command `COPY BOB.TXT \PEOPLE` and Enter. Check the \PEOPLE directory for the BOB.TXT file by typing `DIR \PEOPLE` and Enter.

```
Volume in drive C has no label
Directory of C:\people
.          <DIR>
..         <DIR>
SUE     GRL     31
MARY    GRL     35
JOHN    DOC     45
BOB     TXT     41
    5 file(s)        #### of bytes free
```

Change to the \PEOPLE directory with the command `CD\PEOPLE` and Enter. You'll see the prompt **C:\PEOPLE>**. Now delete the two files with the .GRL extension (SUE.GRL and MARY.GRL) from the \PEOPLE directory with the command (followed by an Enter):

```
DEL *.GRL
```

List the files in the \PEOPLE directory with `DIR` and Enter. As you can see, you've deleted the two files that had the extension .GRL. Remember that the asterisk (wildcard) on the left side of the period takes the place of any or all eight characters in the filename. Therefore, the computer searched for all files with .GRL extension and deleted them.

Now copy the files from the root directory back into the \PEOPLE directory. From the \PEOPLE directory, type COPY *.GRL and Enter. See if the *.GRL files are there using the DIR command.

Make a new file called 1$BY%_3$.&Z! in the \PEOPLE directory with the command COPY CON 1$BY%_3$.&Z! and Enter. (Watch out; this is a very difficult name to type.) Now type the following lines, ending each one with an Enter:

```
It would be nice if there was an easy way to
copy and/or delete it.
^Z
```

Check the \PEOPLE directory to be sure the file was created by typing DIR and Enter. It would be drudgery to type that nasty filename again, so you can copy it to the root directory the easy way, with the command:

```
COPY 1*.* \
```

and Enter. This command statement will copy all the files in the \PEOPLE directory with a number 1 as the first filename character to the root directory. Because you should have only one file with the number 1 as the first filename character, however, you've copied only one file.

Check the root directory to see if it's there by typing DIR \ and Enter. It's there all right. Now you have it in two directories and you want to get rid of both of them.

 Deleting files using wildcards (*) can easily turn into a nightmare. To reduce the chance of accidentally deleting a group of files you don't want to delete, follow the following method when using wildcards.

First, use the DIR command with wildcards to list the group of files you want to delete:

```
DIR 1*.*
```

and Enter. You can see the group of files you'll be deleting in the listing. Now use the DEL command to delete the group of files, with the command:

```
DEL 1*.*
```

and Enter. Use the DIR command to be sure the files are gone. They are!

Now get rid of the nasty file that's in the root directory. Change to the root directory by typing CD \ and Enter. You'll see the **C:\>** prompt. Now list the file to delete in the root directory with the command:

```
DIR 1*.*
```

and Enter. If you're satisfied with the listing, delete the files with:

```
DEL 1*.*
```

and Enter. Now list the files in the root directory to be sure it's gone by typing DIR and Enter. It's gone!

When you have two floppy drives, you can copy a file from one floppy to a second floppy simply by inserting your source disk (the one with the file you want to copy) in drive A:, and your destination disk (where you want to copy the file) in drive B:. Then use the command:

```
COPY filename A: B:
```

DOS will also let you copy a file from a disk in drive A: to another disk, even if you have only one floppy drive. You probably won't use this very often, so the following exercise is optional.

Insert a disk that has files on it into your A: drive, and change to drive A: by typing A: and Enter. To copy all the files on drive A:, enter the following command statement:

```
COPY *.* B:
```

and Enter, and you'll get the following message:

```
Insert diskette for drive B: and strike
any key when ready
```

Remove the disk from drive A: and insert a formatted blank disk in the same floppy drive. Hit the Enter key and the files from the first disk will be copied to the formatted blank disk. Then you'll get the following message:

```
Insert diskette for drive A: and strike
any key when ready
```

Put the original diskette back into drive A:. Hit the Enter key again, and you'll be back to the **A)** prompt if the COPY procedure is complete. Otherwise, you might have to repeat the previous steps until the copying is finished.

The MOVE command (only in MS-DOS version 6.0) can save you much work and time by eliminating the need to go back and delete the original files you just copied.

You have two directories: \NAMES and \PEOPLE. You also have two files in the \PEOPLE directory (MARY.GRL and SUE.GRL) and you want to move them to the \NAMES directory. Try typing the following:

```
MOVE \PEOPLE\*.GRL \NAMES
```

Copying a file between floppy disks

The MOVE command

Situation one

and Enter, and you'll see the following DOS statements on your screen, indicating that the two files that were in the \PEOPLE directory have been moved to the \NAMES directory:

```
c:\people\mary.grl => c:\names\mary.grl [ok]
c:\people\sue.grl  => c:\names\sue.grl [ok]
```

Just to be sure, type:

```
DIR \NAMES
```

and Enter. Now you know the files have been moved to the \NAMES directory. You might also want to check and see if the moved files were deleted from the \PEOPLE directory. Type the command:

```
DIR \PEOPLE
```

and Enter—it looks like the MOVE command really worked! The files JOHN.TXT and BOB.TXT are getting a little lonely all by themselves in the \PEOPLE directory, so why don't you move MARY.GRL and SUE.GRL back. Issue the command:

```
MOVE \NAMES\*.GRL \PEOPLE
```

and Enter. You'll see:

```
c:\names\mary.grl => c:\people\mary.grl [ok]
c:\names\sue.grl  => c:\people\sue.grl [ok]
```

Checking the \PEOPLE directory will show you that the files are back:

```
   Volume in drive C has no label
   Directory of C:\PEOPLE
   .           <DIR>
   ..          <DIR>
SUE      GRL       31
MARY     GRL       35
JOHN     DOC       45
BOB      TXT       41
      6 file(s)        #### of bytes free
```

Is this fun or what?

Situation two Sue, Mary, John, and Bob entered a state lottery and won a million dollars each, they should be in a directory with a more suitable name. You can use the MOVE command to rename a directory. Change the name of the \PEOPLE directory to \WINNERS by typing MOVE \PEOPLE \WINNERS and Enter. You'll see:

```
c:\people => c:\winners [ok]
```

This DOS message indicates that the directory name change was successful.

The PATH command can save you a lot of time and work by eliminating the need to type the full path to program files you want to execute. A path in a computer is a course or route that the computer follows when it's looking for an executable file.

- A directory is an area on a disk used to separate a group of related files from unrelated files (p. 38).
- DOS program files are located in the \DOS directory (p. 45).
- The root directory is the starting point for all other directories, and is designated by the backslash (p. 43).
- You must format new floppy diskettes before they can be used (p. 41).

What you should already know

PATH C:*directory1*; D:*directory2*;*etc.*

Enter the following PATH command, as shown in FIG. 20-1, at the **C:\\>** prompt:

```
PATH C:\;C:\DOS
```

Now, say you decide to format a floppy disk. (Don't worry about this command now; it's explained in the following chapter.) Type the command:

```
FORMAT A:
```

at the **C:\\>** prompt and Enter. The computer immediately looks in the current directory, which in this case is the root directory, for the

**The command
How the PATH command works**

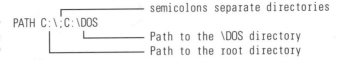

FORMAT.COM file. The computer doesn't find the FORMAT.COM file in the root directory, so it looks at the path to find out where to look next. The PATH command tells the computer to look in the root directory first, and then in the \DOS directory. So the computer looks in the \DOS directory for the FORMAT.COM file, finds it, and runs it so you can format a disk.

What happens if there's no path? If you entered the command:

```
FORMAT A:
```

and Enter, the computer would begin looking in the current directory, which in this case is the root directory, for the FORMAT.COM file. When the file isn't found, the following message would be displayed:

```
Bad command or file name
```

The FORMAT.COM file isn't found because it isn't in the current directory, and there's no path to any other directory. However, with the following typical PATH command:

```
PATH=C:\;C:\DOS
```

the computer will search the root directory and then the \DOS directory for executable program files. Now try typing just the following:

```
PATH
```

at the **C:\\>** prompt. You'll see:

```
PATH=C:\;C:\DOS
```

The PATH command by itself displays the existing path. Entering a new PATH command replaces the old one. For example, if you type:

```
PATH=A:\
```

and Enter, the path now goes to the root directory of drive A:. To display the existing path, type:

```
PATH
```

and Enter, and you'll see:

```
PATH=A:\
```

Avoiding PATH command problems

You can specify a path to many different drives and directories, as long as you separate them with a semicolon. Just remember that the more places the computer needs to look, the longer it will take. Because you can have files with the exact same names in different directories, the wrong file could be executed, causing problems. For example, suppose you enter the following command:

```
PATH=C:\DOS;C:\WP;C:\WS
```

You now have a path to the DOS, WordPerfect, and WordStar directories, in that order. Assume that a file with the name MENU.EXE exists in the WordStar and WordPerfect directories. You're in the root directory and you type the word MENU and Enter. The computer will first look in the current directory and not see the MENU file, so it will follow the path and look in the \DOS directory but still not find the menu file. The computer will then continue along the path to the \WP directory, find the file with the name MENU, and execute it. But what if you wanted to execute a file called MENU in the WordStar directory?

Keep your PATH commands as short as possible. Here's another example of a long PATH statement:

```
PATH=C:\;C:\NAMES;C:\DOS;C:\PEOPLE
```

Using this path, if you typed the command:

```
DISKCOPY A: A:
```

and Enter from the **C:\>** prompt, several things will happen. The root directory will first be searched for the DISKCOPY.COM file. If it isn't found, the computer will then search the C:\NAMES directory for the file. If it isn't found there, the computer will search the C:\DOS directory, where it will find the file and execute it. Because the DISKCOPY.COM file is found and executed from the \DOS directory, the computer won't continue to look in the \PEOPLE directory.

When you specify a path, always list the directories and drives in the order you want them to be searched. I recommend that floppy drives not be included in a PATH statement because the computer might search a floppy drive when it has no disk in it, which will give you an error message.

The map in FIG. 20-2 represents the root directory of your hard drive, each state represents a directory, and each person represents a file. A large number of people are in each state, or you could say a large number of files are in each directory.

A story to explain the PATH command

Now for the PATH command. Let's say you have a brother named FRANK.COM in Florida, a sister named CATHY.EXE in California, and a cousin named TOM.EXE in Texas, and considering you just won 40 million dollars in the Lotto, you ask your friend Joe Computer to get FRANK.COM, CATHY.EXE, and TOM.EXE and bring them to your party.

Without a map (path) like the one in FIG. 20-2, Joe Computer wouldn't have any idea where to look for these people. So what should you do? Give him a

USA = Hard drive (root)
STATES = Directories

20-2
Comparing a map of the United States to a hard drive to illustrate how the PATH command works.

\CALIF
CATHY.EXE

\TEXAS
TOM.EXE

\FLORIDA
FRANK.COM

map that indicates which states to look in. The computer follows the PATH command so it knows which directories to look in. If you entered the following PATH command:

```
PATH=C:\FLORIDA;C:\CALIF;C:\TEXAS
```

Joe Computer would know to look in the states \FLORIDA, \CALIF, and \TEXAS for the people FRANK.COM, CATHY.EXE, and TOM.EXE.

Joe Computer will look only in the directories that the PATH command says to look in, and he can find any executable file in any of those directories.

21 FORMAT & UNFORMAT

You must format all floppy and hard disks when they're new. The term *initialized* means the same as *formatted*. Appendix A, *Loading DOS*, describes how to format a hard drive. This chapter will explain how to format floppy disks.

It's necessary to format floppy disks because your system will read and write only to a formatted floppy disk. Formatting the floppy disk divides the surface into tracks and sectors, similar to the way an audio record is divided into songs. DOS uses these tracks and sectors to locate the files saved to the floppy disk.

Why format floppy disks?

- The floppy disk goes into the drive with the write-protect tab to the left (p. 13).
- A 360K 5¼-inch floppy drive can format only a 360K floppy disk (p. 11).
- A 1.2Mb 5¼-inch floppy drive can format either 360K or 1.2Mb floppy disks (p. 12).
- A 720K 3½-inch floppy drive can format only 720K floppy disks (p. 12).
- A 1.44Mb 3½-inch floppy drive can format both 720K and 1.44Mb floppy disks (p. 12).
- The PROMPT command will show the current directory in the prompt (p. 54).
- Using the PATH command will enable you to execute the FORMAT.COM file located in the \DOS directory from any drive or directory (p. 89).

What you should already know

The commands

```
FORMAT drive [parameters]
UNFORMAT drive
```

Getting your system ready

Issue the following command to show the current directory:

```
PROMPT $P$G
```

and enter. Also create a path to the \DOS directory:

```
PATH C:\DOS
```

and Enter.

Formatting floppy disks

When you format a floppy disk, you completely erase it, so be sure that you don't accidentally insert the wrong floppy disk. If you're using MS-DOS 5.0 or 6.0 and you accidently format the wrong floppy disk, you can restore the floppy disk to its original condition by using the UNFORMAT command.

If you have a floppy disk that contains many directories, it's usually easier to erase the floppy disk using the FORMAT command than it is to delete all the files and remove all the directories. I mentioned earlier that you must format all floppy disks before you can use them (unless they're already formatted). You can format a floppy disk as many times as you want without harming it.

The following examples will show formatting 5¼-inch 360K and 1.2Mb (low and high density) floppy disks using DOS 3.3. Feel free to stop at any point and format as many floppy disks as you like. Begin formatting a floppy disk in a 360K drive. If you don't have one, then skip to the lesson using a 1.2Mb floppy drive.

Formatting a 5¼-inch 360K floppy disk

At the **C:**, type:

```
FORMAT A:
```

and Enter. You'll see the following on screen:

```
Insert new floppy disk for drive a:
and strike ENTER when ready
```

Put the 360K floppy disk in the 360K drive A: and hit Enter. You'll see the following:

```
Head: 0 Cylinder: 0
```

The first 0 will cycle between 0 and 1, and the second number will increase until it reaches 40, and then you'll see:

```
Format complete
    362496 bytes total disk space
    362496 bytes available on disk

Format another (Y/N)?
```

To format another floppy disk, hit the Y key and Enter, and you'll see:

```
Insert new floppy disk for drive a:
and strike ENTER when ready
```

Put the 360K floppy disk in drive A:, hit Enter, and you'll see the Head:/Cylinder: display and then the Format Complete display. To stop formatting, type N and hit Enter, and you'll see the **C:\>** prompt again.

At the **C:\>** prompt, type:

```
FORMAT A:
```

***Formatting a
1.2Mb
floppy disk***

and Enter, and you'll see:

```
Insert new floppy disk for drive a:
and strike ENTER when ready
```

Put the 1.2Mb floppy disk in the 1.2Mb drive A:, hit Enter, and you'll see the following display:

```
Head: 0 Cylinder: 0
```

The first of these numbers will cycle between 0 and 1, the second number will increase until it reaches 80, and then you'll see:

```
Format complete
    1213952 bytes total disk space
    1213952 bytes available on disk

Format another (Y/N)?
```

To format another floppy disk, type Y, hit Enter, and then repeat the previous steps. To stop formatting, type N and hit Enter.

You must use the /4 switch if you want to format a 360K floppy disk in a 1.2Mb high-density drive using DOS 3.3. Use the command:

```
FORMAT A: /4
```

***Formatting a
360K floppy disk
in a 1.2Mb
floppy drive***

and Enter. Insert your disk, hit Enter again, and you'll see the Head:/Cylinder: display. Then you'll see the following:

```
Format complete
    362496 bytes total disk space
    362496 bytes available on disk

Format another (Y/N)?
```

When formatting a 360K floppy disk in a 1.2Mb drive using DOS 5.0 or 6.0, use the /f:360 switch:

```
FORMAT A: /f:360
```

and Enter. Insert your 360K disk, press Enter, and you'll see the following display:

```
Checking existing disk format.
Saving UNFORMAT information.
Verifying 360K.
Format complete.

Volume label (11 characters, ENTER for none)?
```

Hit Enter, and you'll see:

```
362496 bytes total disk space
362496 bytes available on disk
  1024 bytes in each allocation unit.
   354 allocation units available on disk.
Volume Serial Number is ####-####

Format another (Y/N)?
```

Using the UNFORMAT command

The UNFORMAT command is available in MS-DOS 5.0 or 6.0. If you accidently format the wrong floppy disk, the UNFORMAT command can restore the floppy disk to its original condition.

Imagine that you've been working on a proposal for four hours and it's 2:00 a.m., so you save the proposal on a floppy disk in drive A: to take to work. You're extremely tired, but, for some odd reason, decide to format one more floppy disk before you go to bed. You type FORMAT A: and hit the Enter key. When the floppy disk is finished formatting you remove it from the drive and notice that you blindly formatted the floppy disk that your proposal was on. Now what?

You can UNFORMAT the floppy disk you just formatted using DOS 5.0 or 6.0. At the **C:\\>** prompt, type:

```
UNFORMAT A:
```

and Enter. You'll see:

```
Insert disk to rebuild in drive A:
and press ENTER when ready.
```

Place the floppy disk in floppy drive A: and hit Enter. You'll see the following warning:

```
This command should be used only to recover from the
inadvertent use of the FORMAT command. Any other use of the
UNFORMAT command may cause you to lose data! Files modified
since the MIRROR image file was created may be lost.
```

followed by the following information:

```
Searching disk for MIRROR image.
The last time the MIRROR or FORMAT command was used was at
time on date.
```

```
The MIRROR image file has been validated.
Are you sure you want to update the system area of your
drive A (Y/N)?Y
The system area of drive A has been rebuilt.
You may need to restart the system.
```

The floppy disk will now contain all the directories and files it had before you
accidently formatted it. If you accidentally format the wrong floppy disk, use
the UNFORMAT command immediately. The mirror image file that contains
the UNFORMAT information will be overwritten with information from the
next floppy disk you format.

The following command statements will format 3½-inch floppy disks in
various situations. To format a 720K floppy disk in a 720K drive B:, type:

*Other
FORMAT
command
statements*

```
FORMAT B:
```

and Enter. To format a 1.44Mb floppy disk in a 1.44Mb drive A:, type:

```
FORMAT A:
```

and Enter. To format a 720K floppy disk in a 1.44Mb drive A: using DOS 3.3,
type:

```
FORMAT A: /t:80 /n:9
```

And Enter and: (using DOS 5.0 and 6.0)

```
FORMAT A: /f:720
```

and Enter.

You can create a floppy disk that will boot your system by adding the /S
switch to your FORMAT command statement. The /S switch, used with the
FORMAT command, adds the DOS system files to the disk after it's
formatted. These files are two hidden system files and the COMMAND.COM
file, which are always contained in the root directory. You can make a floppy
system disk from any type of floppy disk.

*Bootable
floppy disks*

To make a 1.2Mb floppy system disk in drive A: using DOS 3.3, type:

```
FORMAT A: /s
```

and Enter at the C:\> drive. You'll see:

```
Insert new floppy disk for drive a:
and strike ENTER when ready
```

When the format is complete, you'll see:

```
1213952 bytes total disk space
  69120 bytes used by system
1144832 bytes available on disk

Format another (Y/N)?
```

To stop formatting, type N and hit Enter. Now put your new floppy system disk into drive A: and hit the reset button, or hold the Ctrl and Alt keys down and press the Del key. Your system will boot up, and you'll end up with the **A>** prompt on the screen.

You should always have a couple system floppy disks like the one you just made. If a system file accidentally gets deleted from your hard drive or if your hard drive develops a problem, you'll probably need a floppy system disk to boot your computer. Another valuable reason to have a few bootable floppy disks is that your computer could become infected with a virus. You could then use the clean system files on your bootable floppy disk to replace the contaminated ones on your hard drive.

It's also a good idea to make copies of the files in your \DOS directory onto one or more of your floppy systems disks, in case you need to use any of your DOS utilities and there's a problem with your hard drive.

Bad sectors when formatting

Tracks are divided into sectors. When formatting a floppy disk, the computer finds and locks out sectors that can't be used for storing data. If you try to format a floppy disk that has bad sectors, you'll see a display something like the following at the end of the FORMAT process:

```
362496 bytes total disk space
 20480 bytes in bad sectors
342016 bytes available on disk

Format another (Y/N)?
```

In this previous example, 20480 bytes are contained in bad sectors. If you have a floppy disk that shows bad sectors, try formatting it again. If the bad sectors are still there, it's a good idea to identify the disk as having defective sectors. You can use the faulty floppy disk, but not with the DISKCOPY command because it will write to the bad sectors, causing errors when the floppy disk is read. It's a good idea, however, not to use such a disk at all.

22 DISKCOPY

You can copy one floppy disk, called the *source* floppy disk, to another floppy disk, called the *target* floppy disk, using the DISKCOPY command. The main benefit of using the DISKCOPY command is that hidden, system, and read-only files are copied to the target floppy disk. It's also easier than using the COPY command when you have a floppy disk that contains several subdirectories.

Use the DISKCOPY command when you want an exact duplicate of a floppy disk. The copy you make will have all the directories, subdirectories, and files—just like the source floppy disk. The source floppy disk won't change in the process.

Use the DISKCOPY command to make copies of your software programs, and use the copies to install the software. Should your copies become damaged or erased during installation, you'll still have your originals, which you can copy again.

Why use DISKCOPY?

- The first floppy drive is drive A:, the second floppy drive is drive B:, and the hard drive is drive C:.
- 360K and 720K floppy disks are DSDD (double sided double density) (p. 11–12).
- 1.2Mb and 1.44Mb floppy disks are high density (p. 11–12).

What you should already know

- The `PROMPT $P$G` command will display the current directory in the prompt (p. 55).
- The PATH command allows the computer to follow a route to specified directories (p. 89).

The command

`DISKCOPY sourcedisk targetdisk`

Drives & floppy disks

You can copy a floppy disk of a particular size and density only to a blank disk of the same size and density. For example, you must diskcopy a 5¼-inch 360K disk to a 5¼-inch 360K disk, and a 3½-inch 1.44Mb disk to another 3½-inch 1.44Mb disk.

The type of floppy drives you have on your computer will of course determine which floppy disks you can diskcopy:

- If your system has one 5¼-inch 360K floppy drive, you can use the DISKCOPY command to copy a 360K floppy disk in drive A: to a 360K floppy disk in drive A:.
- If your system has one 5¼-inch 1.2Mb floppy drive, you can use DISKCOPY to copy a 1.2Mb floppy disk in drive A: to a 1.2Mb floppy disk in drive A:, or a 360K floppy disk in drive A: to a 360K floppy disk in drive A:.
- If your system has a 1.2Mb drive A: and a 360K drive B:, you can use DISKCOPY to copy a 360K floppy disk in drive A: to a 360K floppy disk in drive A:, a 360K floppy disk in drive B: to a 360K floppy disk in drive B:, a 1.2Mb floppy disk in drive A: to a 1.2Mb floppy disk in drive A:, a 360K floppy disk in drive A: to a 360K floppy disk in drive B:, and a 360K floppy disk in drive B: to a 360K floppy disk in drive A:.
- If your system has a 1.44Mb floppy drive, you can use DISKCOPY to copy a 1.44Mb floppy disk in drive A: to a 1.44Mb floppy disk in drive A:, and a 720K floppy disk in drive A: to a 720K floppy disk in drive A:.
- If your system has a 1.44Mb drive A: and a 720k floppy drive B: you can use the DISKCOPY command to copy a 1.44Mb floppy disk in drive A: to a 1.44Mb floppy disk in drive A:, a 720K floppy disk in drive A: to a 720K floppy disk in drive A:, a 720K floppy disk in drive B: to a 720K floppy disk in drive B:, a 720K floppy disk in drive A: to a 720K floppy disk in drive B:, and a 720K floppy disk in drive B: to a 720K floppy disk in drive A:.

Note: Remember that you can't diskcopy a high-density floppy to a 360K floppy (DSDD) or vise versa.

DISKCOPY exercises

For the following DISKCOPY exercises, you'll need a source floppy disk (original) with software on it and a target floppy disk (to be the copy). The target floppy disk needs to be formatted, and any information on it will be erased during the DISKCOPY process. I recommend that you put a write-protect tab on your source floppy disks to prevent erasure just in case you accidentally insert the wrong floppy disk.

To begin with, enter the command statement to view the current directory in the prompt by typing:

```
PROMPT $P$G
```

and Enter at the **C>** prompt. Then enter the PATH command that allows you to execute the DISKCOPY.COM file (in the \DOS directory) from the root directory. Type:

```
PATH C:\DOS
```

and Enter at the **C:\>** prompt. For the next exercise, choose the exercise that describes the type of floppy drives in your system.

To diskcopy a 360K floppy disk to another 360K floppy disk, type:

```
DISKCOPY A: A:
```

One 360K floppy drive

and Enter at the **C:\>** prompt. You'll see the following:

```
Insert SOURCE floppy disk in drive A:
Press any key when ready . . .
```

Put your 360K source floppy disk in drive A: and hit a key. The drive light will come on and the computer will start copying the data from the floppy disk into RAM (memory) and you'll see the following message:

```
Copying 40 tracks
9 Sectors/Track, 2 Side(s)
```

When the computer has read as much information into RAM that it can, it will display the following message:

```
Insert TARGET floppy disk in drive A:
Press any key when ready . . .
```

Now put your 360K target floppy disk into drive A: and hit a key. The drive light will come on and the data in RAM that was copied from the source floppy disk to RAM will be copied to the target floppy disk. When copying is complete, you'll get the following message:

```
Copy another floppy disk (Y/N)?
```

If you want to copy another floppy disk, type Y and hit the Enter key, or type the letter N to quit.

When copying 1.2Mb to 1.2Mb floppy disks in drive A:, you'll need to switch floppy disks at least three times because the RAM will hold only about 40% of the source data each time the drive reads it. Start the process by typing:

One 1.2Mb floppy drive

```
DISKCOPY A: A:
```

and Enter at the **C:\>** prompt. You'll see the following:

```
Insert SOURCE floppy disk in drive A:
Press any key when ready . . .
```

Insert your 1.2Mb floppy source disk in drive A: and hit a key. The drive light will come on, the computer will start copying the data from the floppy disk into RAM (memory), and you'll see the following message:

```
Copying 80 tracks
15 Sectors/Track, 2 Side(s)
```

Then you'll be asked to:

```
Insert TARGET floppy disk in drive A:
Press any key when ready . . .
```

Put your 1.2Mb target floppy disk into drive A: and hit a key. The drive light will come on and the data in RAM that was copied from the source floppy disk will be copied to the target floppy disk. When copying is complete, you'll get the following message:

```
Insert SOURCE floppy disk in drive A:
Press any key when ready . . .
```

Reinsert the 1.2Mb source floppy disk in drive A: and hit a key. Keep reinserting the target and source floppy disks until all the information has been copied. When you're done, the following message will appear:

```
Copy another floppy disk (Y/N)?
```

If you want to copy another floppy disk, type a Y and hit Enter, or type N to quit.

A 1.2Mb & 360K floppy drive

This is the best system if you are going to copy a large number of 360K floppy disks. As you'll see, using two drives is the easiest and fastest method of diskcopying. It's best to put the 360K source floppy disk in the 1.2Mb drive and copy to the target floppy disk in the 360K drive. Start with the following command:

```
DISKCOPY A: B:
```

and Enter. You'll be asked to:

```
Insert SOURCE floppy disk in drive A:
Insert TARGET floppy disk in drive B:
Press any key when ready . . .
```

Put your source floppy disk in drive A: and the target floppy disk in drive B: and hit a key. You'll see the message:

```
Copying 40 tracks
9 Sectors/Track, 2 Side(s)
```

The drive A: light will come on as the data from the source floppy disk is copied to RAM, and the drive B: light will come on as the data in RAM is copied to the target floppy disk. Finally, you'll see the following message:

```
Copy another floppy disk (Y/N)?
```

If you want to copy another floppy disk, type a Y and hit the Enter key; if not, type the letter N.

Having one 1.2Mb and one 1.44Mb floppy drive on one computer is the most popular configuration. Unfortunately, you can't use DISKCOPY between the two drives. If your computer has two 1.2Mb floppy drives or two 1.44Mb floppy drives, you can diskcopy from drive A: to drive B: without having to constantly swap between source and target floppy disks.

23 BACKUP

DOS provides an easy way to back up your hard drive. The more important your data, the more important it is to back up your hard drive. You can back up your hard drive to either floppy disks or a magnetic tape drive. If your data is irreplaceable, it's a good idea to make a second backup on floppy disks and store it in a safe place, so a five couldn't destroy both copies. I also print out hard copies of documents for further security.

Why back up the hard drive?

A hard drive, which is an electromechanical device, can last, on average, from three to five years. On the other hand, if defective, it could fail after only a few minutes. When it fails (called a *crash*), all data on the hard drive is gone forever! DOS provides the BACKUP command to enable you to copy all the data from your hard drive to floppy disks and then restore the data from the floppy disks to another hard drive.

What you should already know

- A hard disk and hard drive are the same thing (p. 10).
- You must format new floppy disks with the FORMAT command (p. 41).
- A path to the \DOS directory will allow you to execute the BACKUP command from any drive or directory (p. 89).
- The complement of the BACKUP command is the RESTORE command.
- A forward slash, /, is the indicator for a *switch*, which tells the computer that you want the command to do something additional—for example, BACKUP /s means back up all subdirectories (p. 41).

```
BACKUP sourcedrive targetdrive [switches]
```

Note: The BACKUP and RESTORE commands are a little difficult to use when you're backing up only one file or directory. The reason for this is that the BACKUP and RESTORE commands don't follow typical DOS logic.

Note: If you're using MS-DOS 6.0, skip to the section *MSBACKUP (MS-DOS 6.0 only)*.

The first thing you must do is check your hard drive to see how many megabytes are occupied with data. Use the check disk command (CHKDSK) with the /f switch, followed by the letter of the drive. Type:

```
CHKDSK /f C:
```

and Enter. You'll see the following display:

```
Volume Serial Number is 260C-14F8

 66928640 bytes total disk space
     5238 bytes in 15 directories
 11115553 bytes in 354 user files
 55813087 bytes available on disk

     8192 bytes in each allocation unit
     8170 total allocation units on disk
     6813 available allocation units on disk

   655360 total bytes memory (640K RAM)
   117408 bytes free
```

Let's assume this hard drive is yours, you have approximately 11 megabytes filled with data in 354 user files, and you have a 1.2Mb high-density floppy drive. Each high-density floppy disk will hold approximately 1Mb of information. Because you have 11 megabytes to back up, you'll need approximately 11 high-density floppy disks. Be sure to format at least 11 floppy disks. You must format the floppy disks used with the BACKUP command first if you're using DOS 3.3 or earlier. DOS 4.01 and 5.0 will format the floppy disk during the BACKUP procedure. If you're using a 360K (DSDD) floppy drive, you'll need approximately 37 floppy disks (3.3 times as many).

First, change to the \DOS directory by typing:

```
CD \DOS
```

and Enter at the **C:\>** prompt. Then type:

```
BACKUP C:\ A: /s /l
```

and Enter at the **C:\DOS>** prompt. This command statement will start the BACKUP in the root directory of drive C: and send all the files to drive A:, including all directories and subdirectories.

The /s switch specifies to back up subdirectories, and the /l switch tells BACKUP to create an ASCII file named BACKUP.LOG in the root directory of the drive you're backing up. The BACKUP.LOG file contains a complete list of the files backed up and what floppy disk they're on. Once you've entered the command, you'll be prompted to:

```
Insert backup diskette 01 in drive A:
```

and given the following warning:

```
Warning! Files in the target drive
A:\ root directory will be erased
Press any key to continue . . .
```

Put a floppy disk in drive A: and hit a key to start the process. You'll see the filenames preceded by their directories listed on the monitor as they're copied onto the floppy disk.

One of the wonderful things about the BACKUP procedure is that it records the filenames and the directories they're in. When you use the RESTORE procedure to copy the backup floppy disks to another hard drive, the complete directory structure is automatically recreated and all the files are placed where they belong. Your new hard drive should contain the same files and directories as your old hard drive.

Backing up files in one directory

Sometimes, you want or need to back up only specific files or directories. Suppose you have all your original Lotus 1-2-3 program floppy disks and don't mind reinstalling them if your hard drive crashes. You're creating a series of spreadsheets using Lotus 1-2-3 to help you track production and costs in your pizza business. Your Lotus 1-2-3 program files are located in the directory \123 and your spreadsheets are located in the subdirectory \123\PIZZA. You want to back up the \123\PIZZA directory where your spreadsheets are located. Put a formatted floppy disk in drive A:, and type:

```
BACKUP C:\123\PIZZA A: /s /l
```

and Enter at the **C:\DOS>** prompt. Put a floppy disk in drive A: and hit a key to start the process. You'll see the spreadsheet files listed on the monitor as they're copied onto the floppy disks. The /l switch will cause the BACKUP.LOG file to be updated with the date and time of the backup and the floppy disk number, followed by the directories and filenames on that floppy disk. The prompt will appear when the backup is complete.

Use the TYPE command and the MORE filter (p. 62) to create a listing of the BACKUP.LOG file:

```
TYPE C:\BACKUP.LOG | MORE
```

and Enter. You'll see the following on screen:

```
10-23-1991 17:42:20
001 \123\PIZZA\INV204.WK1
```

```
001 \123\PIZZA\INV206.WK1
001 \123\PIZZA\INV207.WK1
001 \123\PIZZA\INV208.WK1
001 \123\PIZZA\INV209.WK1
001 \123\PIZZA\INV210.WK1
001 \123\PIZZA\INV213.WK1
001 \123\PIZZA\INV211.WK1
001 \123\PIZZA\INV212.WK1
001 \123\PIZZA\INV214.WK1
001 \123\PIZZA\INV215.WK1
001 \123\PIZZA\INV216.WK1
001 \123\PIZZA\INV217.WK1
001 \123\PIZZA\INV218.WK1
001 \123\PIZZA\INV219.WK1
001 \123\PIZZA\INV220.WK1
---More---

001 \123\PIZZA\INV221.WK1
001 \123\PIZZA\INV222.WK1
001 \123\PIZZA\INV223.WK1
001 \123\PIZZA\INV224.WK1
001 \123\PIZZA\INV225.WK1
001 \123\PIZZA\INV226.WK1
001 \123\PIZZA\INV227.WK1
001 \123\PIZZA\INV228.WK1
001 \123\PIZZA\INV229.WK1
001 \123\PIZZA\INV230.WK1
001 \123\PIZZA\INV231.WK1
001 \123\PIZZA\INV232.WK1
```

Note: 001 is the floppy disk backup number.

When files are backed up, their format is changed. If you're using DOS 3.2 or earlier and you do a DIR of one of the backup floppy disks, you'll see that the filenames look the same as they did on the hard drive before the backup. However, you can't use them until you restore them with the RESTORE command in your \DOS directory.

Each file has its own archive bit. When you first load all your software onto the hard drive, the archive bit is set on. When you back up a file using the BACKUP command, the archive bit is set off (cleared). If you add or modify a file, the archive bit is set on. This is how the computer knows if a file needs to be backed up when you perform a BACKUP update. The BACKUP C:\ A: /s /1 will back up all files, no matter how the archive bit is set. The /m switch, added after the /s, will cause the computer to look at the archive bit and decide which files should be backed up.

If you have a printer, you can make a hardcopy (printout) of your backup by holding down the Ctrl key and hitting the PrtSc (print screen) key. When you do this, everything that prints on the monitor screen will also print on the

Things you should know

printer. You'll have a listing of each file, the directory the file is in, and the number of the backup floppy disk the file is on. To turn this printing feature off, hold down the Ctrl key and hit the PrtSc key again. If you use the /l switch, you can later send the BACKUP.LOG file (located in the root directory of the drive that was backed up to the screen) to either the screen or the printer (or both) with the TYPE command.

BACKUP update

After the entire hard drive is backed up, you'll probably want to back up new documents and files and/or old documents and files you have modified. This should be done as often as you feel necessary, but surely at the end of each day. You do this by adding a couple of switches to the BACKUP command.

Imagine that you just backed up the entire hard drive and have written a letter to your friend. Now you want a backup (copy) of the letter on a floppy disk, but you don't want to back up the whole hard drive again. You also want to back up other new or modified files since the full backup was done. You want to do a BACKUP update.

You must use the last floppy disk from your full backup as backup update floppy disk #1. If you try using a blank floppy disk, the computer will loop and keep asking for you to insert the last backup floppy disk. Put the last floppy disk from your full backup in drive A: and type the following at the **C:\DOS>** prompt:

```
BACKUP C:\ A: /s /m /a /l
```

When you hit the Enter key, the computer starts looking for files in the root directory of drive C: that have their archive bits set to on. Those files are backed up to the floppy disk and then their archive bits are set to off.

The /a switch tells the computer to add to the floppy disk in drive A:. When you do a full backup, each floppy disk is erased before written to. When you do a BACKUP update, you start with your last full backup floppy disk and you keep adding to it until it's full. When it is full, a message will come on the monitor telling you to insert another floppy disk into drive A:.

The /l switch by itself will create a file named BACKUP.LOG in the root directory of the drive you're backing up. You can specify a filename other than BACKUP.LOG. Suppose you wanted to call the file RICKS.BAK and always put it in the root directory of drive C:, you'd type:

```
BACKUP C:\ A: /s /l:C:\RICKS.BAK
```

and Enter. You should always have extra blank formatted floppy disks in case you have underestimated the number needed to do the backup, which is usually the case. If you want to stop the backup process, hold down the Ctrl key and hit the letter C. Every time a file is backed up, the archive bit is set to off.

If, for some unknown reason, your computer won't recognize your last full backup floppy disk, you can quickly make one using the full BACKUP command, BACKUP C:\ A: /s. After four or five files have been backed up to the floppy disk in floppy drive A:, hold down the Ctrl key and hit the letter C. This will terminate the backup procedure and the floppy disk in drive A: will be the last backup floppy disk and will be accepted when you do the update.

MSBACKUP is a new backup program included with MS-DOS 6.0 that makes backing up and restoring files much easier. Unlike the older DOS BACKUP command, which requires you to type out the command and a series of switches, MSBACKUP gives you a menu from which you can select various options and commands with a mouse. Automatic configuring and compatibility tests make using this program simple, and help is available any time you need it by pressing the F1 function key. MSBACKUP won't restore backups created with the BACKUP command from MS-DOS 5.0 or earlier. To start MSBACKUP, type the following at the **C:\DOS>** prompt:

MSBACKUP (MS-DOS 6.0)

```
MSBACKUP
```

and Enter. Using either Alt–F or Alt–H will activate the drop-down menus available from the main menu, shown in FIG. 23-1. The first time MSBACKUP is started, it will automatically configure itself to work with your computer. MSBACKUP will format floppy disks as it performs a backup, but if you format the floppy disks before backing up, the backup process will take less time.

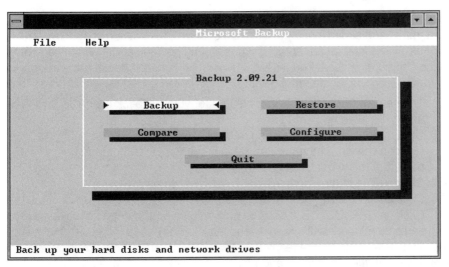

23-1
The MSBACKUP Main Menu, with Backup highlighted.

Imagine that you just upgraded to MS-DOS 6.0 and decide to do a full backup of your hard drive. I'll assume that you're using a mouse, but you'll be able to follow even if you're using the keyboard. Start by typing:

Backing up your entire hard disk

```
MxKUP
```

and Enter at the **C:\DOS>** prompt. Then follow these steps:

1. From the main menu, select Backup (place the arrow on Backup and press the left mouse button).
2. Under the heading Backup From, double-click (two fast clicks of the left mouse button) on the [-C-] to select all files on the C: drive. If you have another hard drive (D: for example), you can select more than one letter.
3. The designation Full should be displayed under the heading Backup Type.
4. The proper floppy disk to back up to should be displayed under the Backup To heading. If not, click on either [-A-] or [-B-], and select the correct floppy drive type.
5. Select File in upper left-hand corner.
6. Select Save Setup As... and type the name of your new setup file. Press the down arrow on the keyboard once.
7. Type *a full backup of all drives* in the Description option.
8. Click on the Save button.

At this point, you'll be taken back to the START BACKUP screen. The name of the file you specified will be shown under the heading Setup File, with the extension .SET. The setup file holds the information you just entered so you don't need to do it again. The next time you want a full backup of your hard drive, just select that setup file. To begin the backup procedure, simply click on Start Backup.

Doing an incremental backup

MSBACKUP also allows you to easily back up just the files that have been modified and added since the last full backup. A full backup should be done once a week and incremental backups should be done at the end of each day the computer is used. You'll need a floppy disk for each day of the week on which to do the incremental backup.

1. The name of the setup file you created for your full backup should be listed under the heading Setup File.
2. Click on Full under the heading Backup Type.
3. Click on the word Incremental. A black dot will be centered in the circle to the left of the word. Click on OK.
4. Click on File in the upper left-hand corner of screen.
5. Click on Save Setup As... with the left mouse button.
6. Click on DEFAULT.SET with the right mouse button or press the spacebar, and a checkmark will appear to the left.
7. Type Alt–C and you're ready to enter a description.
8. Type *modified backup* or *added files*, and click on the Save button.
9. To begin the incremental backup, simply click on the Start Backup button.

Summary

Now that you know how to use the BACKUP command, you need to know how to use the RESTORE command. You must use the RESTORE command to copy the BACKUP floppy disks back to the hard drive. The next chapter describes how to restore these files using the RESTORE command and MSBACKUP.

24 RESTORE

The RESTORE command is the opposite of the BACKUP command. The BACKUP command copies files and directories from the hard drive to floppy disks, and the RESTORE command copies the files and directories from the disks back to the hard drive.

You'll need to restore a floppy-disk backup to your hard drive if the hard drive has crashed. If you accidentally delete a file, you can restore it from your backup disks. You can use RESTORE only with disks that contain files that have been backed with the DOS BACKUP command.

- Backup files on backup disks, when you're using DOS 3.21 or earlier, have normal filenames, but can be used only if they're restored.
- You need to back up because your hard drive will eventually fail (p. 104).
- Typing PATH C:\DOS will enable you to use DOS commands from anywhere in the computer (p. 89).
- A forward slash / followed by certain letters (a switch) is used to tell the computer that you want to do something additional. For example, /s means all subdirectories (p. 41).
- The wildcard specification *.* means all files (p. 44).

RESTORE *backupdisk harddrive*

Why & when to use RESTORE

What you should already know

The command

Note that the RESTORE command causes difficulty for many computer users because it doesn't follow typical DOS logic.

Using the correct version

MS-DOS 6.0 introduced a program called MSBACKUP that backs up and restores using a special file format that isn't compatible with any other version of MS-DOS. MS-DOS 6.0 comes, however, with a RESTORE.EXE file so you can restore backups made with earlier versions of MS-DOS to your computer running MS-DOS 6.0.

For versions of MS-DOS 5.0 and earlier, the RESTORE command works with backup disks created with its own version or earlier versions, but not later versions. For example, if you create a backup from your computer using MS-DOS 2.1 and then upgrade your computer to MS-DOS 3.3, you can restore your old backup to your computer. But if your friend creates a backup using MS-DOS 5.0, you won't be able to restore his backup to your computer running MS-DOS 3.3.

Note: If you've backed up using MSBACKUP in MS-DOS 6.0, skip to the heading *Using RESTORE with MS-DOS 6.0*.

Restoring drive A: to drive C:

The following is an example of one of the most popular ways to use the RESTORE command.

Your hard drive lasted only three months before it irretrievably crashed. You take the computer to your dealer who replaces the hard drive. He formats the hard drive and gives you back the computer. You, being a wise person, have a complete set of backup disks and some backup update disks. You're a little nervous because you created some wonderful files that would be difficult to duplicate if lost. What do you do?

Put your system floppy disk in drive A: and turn the computer on. Once the computer has booted and you have an **A:>** prompt on screen, put your first backup restore disk in the **A:>** prompt and check the disk for the RESTORE.COM file if you're using DOS 4.01 or earlier or the RESTORE.EXE if you're using DOS 5.0 or 6.0. Then type, at the **A:>** prompt:

```
DIR RESTORE.*
```

and Enter. If the RESTORE.COM or RESTORE.EXE file isn't listed, then locate the disk with the RESTORE.COM or RESTORE.EXE file on it and insert it into drive A:.

The next thing is to type in the RESTORE command using the proper switches to get the results you want. You want to restore all the files on the backup disks to drive C: and you want them to be in the same directories as they were when you did the backup. Enter the following command statement at the **A:>** prompt:

```
RESTORE A: C: /s
```

and Enter. The /s means to put the files in their directories. You'll get this message from the computer:

```
Insert backup diskette 01 in drive A:
Press any key to continue...
```

Now remove the DOS disk from drive A:, put in the BACKUP number 01 disk, and hit a key. You'll see the filenames and directories on the monitor as they're being restored to the hard drive.

Note: The disk won't lose data. It can be kept and used again if you need to restore your data again.

When the computer needs disk number two, you'll see the following message:

```
Insert backup diskette 02 in drive A:
Press any key to continue...
```

Continue to insert the backup disks by number as the computer asks for them. When the restoration process is complete, the computer will stop asking for more disks.

I'll bet you're wondering about the backup update disks. Well, here's the scoop. If you started your backup update using the last disk from your original backup, your update disks become part of your original backup and the computer will ask for them by number. If you used Ctrl–C during a full backup to create a last backup disk, then you can use the same RESTORE command explained previously. Just put the backup disks into drive A:, followed by the backup update disks, as the computer asks for them until it stops asking, which means the restoration process is complete.

Now hold down the Ctrl and Alt keys and hit the Del key to warm boot the system, or hit the system reset button (or turn the computer off) for a cold boot. Be sure the floppy drive door is open so the computer boots from the hard drive.

You don't have to restore your whole hard drive if you accidentally delete files from a directory or subdirectory.

Restoring one directory

Say you accidentally erase all the files in your Lotus 1-2-3 directory. Now you want to restore the Lotus 1-2-3 files from your backup disks to your hard drive. Your hard drive has all its other directories and files intact and you have a path to the \DOS directory. What do you do? Enter the following command statement at the **C:\>** prompt:

```
RESTORE A: C:\123\*.* /s
```

and Enter. I recommend always using the /s switch. It will cause all the subdirectories of the \123 directory to also be restored. You'll get the following message:

```
Insert backup diskette 01 in drive A:
Press any key to continue...
```

If you have ten backup disks and you know that the \123 directory is on number 04 disk, then put the number 04 disk into the A: drive instead of the number 01 disk it requests. If you put the number 01 disk in drive A: and hit a key to start the process, you'll be asked to put disk 02 into drive A: when the \123 directory isn't found. You'll then be asked to put in the next higher number disk until the \123 directory is found, at which time the computer will begin restoring the files.

If you put the number 04 disk into drive A: and hit a key to begin the process, you'll get the following message:

```
*** Files were backed up MM/DD/YYYY ***

Warning! Diskette is out of sequence
Replace diskette or continue if OK
Press any key to continue...
```

No problem. Just hit a key to begin the process and your complete directory and subdirectories of files will be restored to the \123 directory.

Note: If you used the /l switch with the BACKUP command when you did your BACKUP, you'll have a BACKUP.LOG file in the root directory of the drive that you backed up. If you TYPE out this file, you can see which files were backed up to which disk. Suppose you wanted to find out which backup disk WordPerfect was backed up on. Type the following at the **C:\>** prompt:

```
TYPE C:\BACKUP.LOG | MORE
```

and Enter. You'll see a listing like the following:

```
10-04-1991  13:20:09
001    \PS\INVITE.PFV
001    \PS\IRISES.PFL
001    \PS\JUKEBOX.PFV
001    \PS\LASSEN.PNF
001    \PS\LAYOUTS.PSF
001    \PS\LIBRARY.PFL
002    \WP51\INSTALL.EXE
002    \WP51\CONVERT.EXE
002    \WP51\GRAPHCONV.EXE
002    \WP51\MACROCNV.EXE
002    \WP51\WPINFO.EXE
002    \WP51\SPELL.EXE
003    \WP51\NWPSETUP.EXE
003    \WP51\WP.EXE
```

As you can see from the listing, WordPerfect began backing up on disk number two.

What if you don't need the whole directory—just one file you destroyed. The RESTORE command can be used here, also.

Restoring one file

Say that a week ago you wrote a detailed report and named it REPORT1.LTR. It's on one of your backup update disks. Today you decide to print it, so you bring it up in WordPerfect 5.1 to make some corrections. After playing around with spacing, different font styles and formatting, you accidentally save it, replacing the original. Knowing how much work it would be to straighten out all the weird things you did to the file, you decide to restore the original version from your BACKUP disks.

If you've been using the /L switch with your BACKUP command, TYPE out the BACKUP.LOG file to see which disk the REPORT1.LTR file is on, otherwise, you will have to start with disk number one, or guess which disk the file might be on. Enter the following command statement at the **C:\>** prompt:

```
RESTORE A: C:REPORT1.LTR /s
```

and Enter. The /s switch is necessary to locate and restore the file in its proper directory structure. You'll get the message:

```
Insert backup diskette 01 into drive A:
Press any key to continue...
```

Simply put the BACKUP disk with the REPORT1.LTR file on it into drive A: and hit a key. If the disk in drive A: isn't the number 01 disk, you'll see the message:

```
*** Files were backed up MM/DD/YYYY ***

Warning! Diskette is out of sequence
Replace diskette or continue if OK
Press any key to continue...
```

Hit a key and the process will begin. Your file will be restored to the \WP51 directory.

Using RESTORE

MS-DOS 6.0 offers two ways to restore files to your hard drive—each using a different RESTORE program.

Restoring backups from previous MS-DOS versions

MS-DOS 6.0 includes a RESTORE.EXE file that enables you to restore any backups you created using the BACKUP command of versions of MS-DOS 5.0 or earlier. This method is explained earlier in this chapter.

MSBACKUP is a new backup program included with MS-DOS 6.0 that restores as well as backs up. When you enter the command MSBACKUP on the command line, a menu (shown in FIG. 24-1) will appear, giving you the choices of BACKUP or RESTORE. Because MSBACKUP has its own special file format, you can restore only files that were backed up with MSBACKUP. If you need help while using MSBACKUP, simply press the F1 function key.

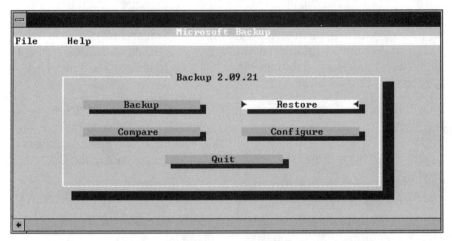

24-1
*The MSBACKUP Main
Menu, with the Restore
function highlighted.*

Say you just finished creating a full backup of your hard drive using MSBACKUP. Of course you put your backup set in a safe place. While you were out, a relative came to visit and decided to play with your computer while he waited for you to come home. Whoops, seems as though he accidentally deleted your favorite game, F15 Strike Eagle. Type the following command at the **C:\>** prompt:

```
MSBACKUP
```

and enter. Then follow these steps:

1. Select RESTORE from the MSBACKUP main menu (use the Tab and Enter keys or point and click with left mouse button) and the Restore main menu will appear (see FIG. 24-2).
2. Under the heading Backup Set Catalog, you need to specify the correct backup set for the files you want. If not, click on the filename with the right mouse button, click on the correct filename, and then click on Load.
3. Under the heading Restore Files, double click on the desired drive letter, C. Double click again and it will toggle between two states: All Files, meaning that all files on the backup disks from that drive letter will be restored, and Select Files, which means you must pick the files you want restored.

4. You don't want to restore all files, just the \F15 directory, so click the left mouse button on Select Files. Double click on the \F15 directory and you'll see check marks next to each filename on the right side of the monitor screen.
5. Click on the OK button.
6. Click on the Start Restore button.
7. The Alert box will appear, telling you which disk to insert into which floppy drive. Insert the correct number disk and click on the Continue button.

Your software has been restored to your hard drive.

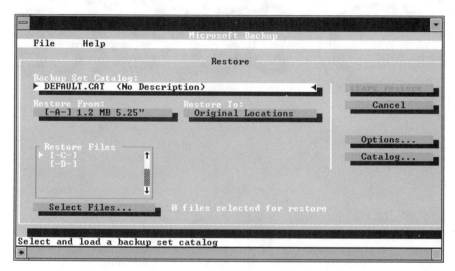

24-2
The MSBACKUP Restore menu.

25 XCOPY & DELTREE

XCOPY.EXE is a program that resides in your \DOS directory. You can access it from any drive or directory if you first establish a path to the \DOS directory. In contrast, the COPY command is always accessible because it resides in the COMMAND.COM file, which is loaded when the computer boots up.

Why use XCOPY?

In most cases, the COPY command is sufficient for copying files, but XCOPY lets you copy a directory and all its subdirectories and files using only one command statement.

What you should already know

- A subdirectory is a directory within another directory (p. 43).
- The PROMPT PG command will make the current directory visible in the prompt (p. 55).
- The PATH command will create a route to specified directories and enable execution of the .COM and .EXE files in those directories (p. 89).
- The MORE filter stops a long screen listing at 25 lines, so the top of the list doesn't scroll by (p. 62).

The command

XCOPY *sourcedirectory targetdirectory*

Using XCOPY

Use the XCOPY command to copy a directory and its subdirectories and files to another computer.

You want to copy the games from your computer to a friend's computer. Both computers have 1.2Mb floppy drives. All the games total less than 1.2Mb in size so they'll fit on one high-density floppy disk (see FIG. 25-1). Insert a formatted 1.2Mb disk in your 1.2Mb floppy drive and type the following at the **C:\>** prompt:

```
XCOPY C:\GAMES A:\GAMES /s /e
```

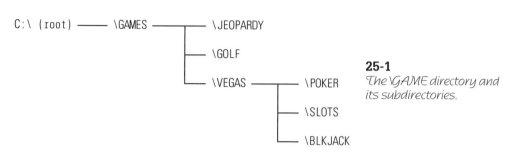

25-1
The \GAME directory and its subdirectories.

```
C:\ (root) ——— \GAMES ———————— \JEOPARDY

                           ├── \GOLF

                           └── \VEGAS ——————— \POKER

                                              ├── \SLOTS

                                              └── \BLKJACK
```

and Enter. The /s means to copy all subdirectories that contain files. If you add an /e switch, it means to copy empty subdirectories as well. You'll get the following message:

```
Does GAMES specify a file name
or directory name on the target.
(F = file, D = directory)?
```

Hit the letter D and DOS will create the directory \GAMES on the floppy in drive A: and fill it with the subdirectories and files that belong there. To copy \GAMES to your friend's computer, place the disk that contains the \GAMES directory in his floppy drive and type the following at the **C:\>** prompt:

```
XCOPY A:\GAMES C:\GAMES /s /e
```

and Enter. You will get the following message:

```
Does GAMES specify a file name
or directory name on the target.
(F = file, D = directory)?
```

Hit the letter D and DOS will create the directory \GAMES on drive C: in your friend's computer and fill it with the subdirectories and files that belong there.

You have two hard drives in your computer, C: and D:. You need more room on drive C:, so you decide to move the \WP51 (WordPerfect 5.1) directory and all its subdirectories to drive D: and then delete the WordPerfect 5.1 program from drive C:. First XCOPY the \WP51 directory to the D: drive by typing the following command at the **C:\>** prompt:

```
XCOPY C:\WP51 D:\WP51 /s /e
```

and Enter. Then run the WordPerfect 5.1 program that was copied to drive D: to be sure it's operating properly, and make sure that all the subdirectories and files were transferred. Then delete the files in the \WP51 directory and subdirectories on drive C: and, using the RD (Remove Directory) command, remove the subdirectories and the \WP51 directory.

Wow! Deleting all those files and removing all those directories sounds like an awful lot of work, and it is. If you're using MS-DOS 6.0, you can use a new command called DELTREE—see later in this chapter.

Situation three Last month you installed your mouse software into the directory \MOUSE and it has worked perfectly. Now you decide to install a newer version of mouse software, but are concerned that the new software, which will overwrite the old software, might not work correctly. XCOPY the old \MOUSE directory to another directory name with the following command:

```
XCOPY C:\MOUSE C:\MOUSE.OLD /s /e
```

Now all the old mouse files are in the \MOUSE.OLD directory. Install the new mouse software into the \MOUSE directory. If you're happy with the performance of the new software, delete the old mouse files and remove the \MOUSE.OLD directory. If you don't want to use the new mouse software, delete the files in the \MOUSE directory and XCOPY the \MOUSE.OLD directory back to the \MOUSE directory:

```
XCOPY C:\MOUSE.OLD C:\MOUSE /s /e
```

Now you have your old mouse software back in the \MOUSE directory and the mouse will operate as before.

More practice with XCOPY Let's make a directory structure and XCOPY it to another directory name and then remove both directory structures. First make a directory named \MONEY. At the **C:\)** prompt, type:

```
MD \MONEY
```

and Enter. Now make two subdirectories, \MONEY\NICKELS and \MONEY\PENNIES:

```
MD \MONEY\NICKELS
```

and Enter, and:

```
MD \MONEY\PENNIES
```

and Enter. You now have a directory structure like the one in FIG. 25-2. You can use XCOPY to make a duplicate directory structure with a different name, like the one in FIG. 25-3. At the **C:\)** prompt, type:

```
XCOPY \MONEY \COINS /s /e
```

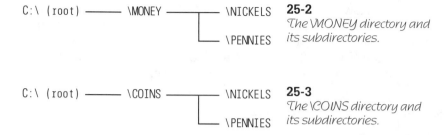

```
C:\ (root) ———— \MONEY ————┬—— \NICKELS
                           └—— \PENNIES
```

25-2
The \MONEY directory and its subdirectories.

```
C:\ (root) ———— \COINS ————┬—— \NICKELS
                           └—— \PENNIES
```

25-3
The \COINS directory and its subdirectories.

and Enter. You'll see the following message:

```
Does COINS specify a file name
or directory name on the target
(F= file, D= directory)
```

Type D and Enter, and you'll see:

```
File not found - ????????.???
          0 File(s) copied
```

You got the error message because there were no files in any of the directories you tried to XCOPY.

If you're using MS-DOS 4.01, 5.0, or 6.0, you can use the TREE command to graphically display the directory structures on a drive. Use the TREE command to look at the directory structures you just made. At the **C:\>** prompt, type:

```
TREE ¦ MORE
```

and Enter. You'll see something like the following (if you have other directories and subdirectories, you'll see them as well):

```
Directory PATH listing for Volume LEARN_DOS
```

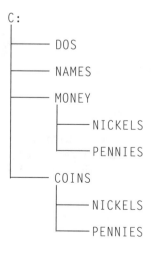

```
C:
├——— DOS
├——— NAMES
├——— MONEY
│       ├———NICKELS
│       └———PENNIES
└——— COINS
        ├———NICKELS
        └———PENNIES
```

Now that you know how to XCOPY directory structures, let's do a little house cleaning and remove the directory structures you just made. If you're using MS-DOS 6.0, skip to the DELTREE command and remove the directory structures the easy way; otherwise, issue the following commands at the **C:** prompt (don't forget the to hit Enter after each one):

```
RD \COINS\PENNIES
RD \COINS\NICKELS
RD \COINS
RD \MONEY\PENNIES
RD \MONEY\NICKELS
RD \MONEY
```

Use the TREE command again and see if the directory structures are gone.

DELTREE (MS-DOS 6.0)

The DOS 6.0 DELTREE command removes a complete directory structure. It can save you a tremendous amount of work, but, if you use it improperly, can turn into a nightmare—so use it with extreme care.

You want to remove the \MONEY and the \COINS directory structures. What would happen if you had the bright idea to use the following command statement at the **C:** prompt (*Do not* type the following command):

```
DELTREE C:\
```

This command would completely remove everything from the root directory of drive C:, so be very careful using the DELTREE command!

Situation one

In order to remove the C:\MONEY and C:\COINS directories, you need to issue the following two command statements from the **C:** prompt (don't forget to follow each with an Enter):

```
DELTREE \MONEY
DELTREE \COINS
```

Now, if you list the tree for the C:\ drive, you'll see that the directory structures are gone.

It would take six command statements with a lower DOS version and, if there were files in each of the directories, it would take twelve separate command statements to remove the two directory structures. I love this command. You will too.

Situation two

You used the XCOPY command to copy a \WP51 directory structure to drive D:, as explained earlier in this chapter, and now you want to remove the old directory structure. Change to the C: drive and, at the **C:** prompt, enter the DELTREE command:

```
DELTREE \WP51
```

and Enter. You'll see the following display:

```
Delete directory "\wp51" and all its subdirectories? [yn]
```

Type Y and Enter, and you'll see:

```
deleting wp51...
```

Situation three

Earlier in this chapter, you used XCOPY to copy a \GAMES directory structure to a floppy disk so you could copy it to a friend's computer. Now you want to remove all the files and directories from the floppy disk. Change to the A: drive and, at the **A:** prompt, type:

```
DELTREE \
```

and Enter. You'll see:

```
Delete directory "\" and all its subdirectories? [yn]
```

Type Y and Enter, and you'll see:

```
deleting \...
```

The disk is now empty. Another way to achieve the same result, although more time consuming, would be to format the disk.

26 CONFIG.SYS & EDIT

The CONFIG.SYS file is the first file that's executed when the computer is turned on (booted). It allows you to configure your system by altering system parameters and loading device drivers. See FIG. 26-1 for an explanation of the name.

26-1
The meaning of the CONFIG.SYS filename and extension.

What is a CONFIG.SYS file?

The CONFIG.SYS file is a system file, and is the only system file you can modify. DOS typically has two hidden system files that are loaded into RAM by the BIOS when the computer is booted. These hidden system files are located in the root directory—you can list them by changing their attributes or, when using MS-DOS 5.0 or 6.0, by using the `DIR /as` command. You can't alter the hidden system files that are loaded by DOS, so the CONFIG.SYS file exists to enable you to modify the default values built into DOS.

What you should already know

- COPY CON means *copy from console* (p. 58).
- Pushing the F6 function key gives you the character ^Z (p. 35).
- The DIR command will list the files in the current (default) directory unless you specify other parameters (p. 51).

- RAM means *random-access memory* (p. 43).
- The PROMPT PG command will make the current directory visible in the prompt (p. 55).
- The PATH command will create a route to selected directories and enable the execution of the files in those directories (p. 89).

The CONFIG.SYS file is an ASCII file that must be located in the root directory of drive C:. You can use the COPY CON command to create it. First change to drive C: and, if you aren't in the root directory, type:

```
CD \
```

and Enter. Now check to see if a CONFIG.SYS file already exists by typing:

```
DIR CONFIG.SYS
```

and Enter. If a CONFIG.SYS file exists, using the command COPY CON CONFIG.SYS will replace the old CONFIG.SYS file with your new one. MS-DOS 5.0 and 6.0 automatically create a CONFIG.SYS file when they're installed, so be careful not to overwrite it. To change an existing file using MS-DOS 5.0 or 6.0, go to the heading *EDIT (MS-DOS 5.0 and 6.0)*.

If no CONFIG.SYS file appears in the directory listing, use the COPY CON command to make a basic CONFIG.SYS file that you can use on any computer with DOS 2.0 or later. Type:

```
COPY CON CONFIG.SYS
```

and Enter. Then type the following lines, following each one with an Enter:

```
buffers=20
files=20
break=on
^Z
```

Now make sure that you created the CONFIG.SYS in the root directory of drive C: by typing DIR and Enter. The file should be there. Now display the CONFIG.SYS file on the monitor screen by typing:

```
TYPE CONFIG.SYS
```

and Enter. You should see the following:

```
buffers=20
files=20
break on
```

Note: When you change or make a new CONFIG.SYS file, you must reboot your computer for the changes to take effect because the CONFIG.SYS file can be loaded only at boot time.

The following is an example of a CONFIG.SYS file that loads MS-DOS 5.0 or 6.0 in the HMA (high-memory area) on a 386 or 486 computer. Type:

```
COPY CON CONFIG.SYS
```

and Enter at the **C:\>** prompt, and then enter the following lines (ending each one by hitting the Enter key):

```
device=C:\DOS\HIMEM.SYS /machine:1
DOS=high,UMB
buffers=20
files=20
break=on
shell=C:\DOS\COMMAND.COM C:\DOS /p
device=C:\DOS\SMARTDRV.SYS 512 256
device=C:\DOS\EMM386.EXE RAM
device=C:\DOS\SETVER.EXE
lastdrive=z
device=C:\DOS\ANSI.SYS
^Z
```

The following is an explanation of several settings in this CONFIG.SYS file:

`HIMEM.SYS` is the extended memory manager. It controls the use of extended memory, so each program has its own memory space, thereby preventing conflicts. The `/machine:1` switch specifies which A20 handler HIMEM.SYS will use to gain access to the HMA. If HIMEM.SYS doesn't load, try another number in place of one, up to 14.

`DOS=high,UMB` loads the DOS system into the HMA, the purpose of which is to free up conventional (base) memory. HIGH tells DOS to load high, and UMB (upper-memory block) links conventional memory with the UMA (upper-memory area), which is 640K to 1Mb.

`Buffers=20` means that 10,560 bytes of memory will be used to store data that's retrieved from a disk drive. This increases access speed to information that has already been retrieved.

`Files=20` means that 20 files can be open at one time. I've come across some software programs that require a minimum of 20 files to be open. Without this statement in the CONFIG.SYS file, these software programs won't run.

`Break=on` will increase your ability to stop programs from running. Typing Ctrl–C or the Break key is how you initiate a break.

`Shell` When installing DOS 5.0 or 6.0, the setup program automatically installs the SHELL command into the CONFIG.SYS file, which is why I've included it here. As long as the COMMAND.COM file is in the root directory, you can omit this command statement. SHELL specifies which command processor (COMMAND.COM) is going to be used and where it's located. I prefer using the SHELL command in the following CONFIG.SYS sample file.

The next sample CONFIG.SYS file loads DOS 5.0 or 6.0 into the HMA, and device drivers into the UMA on a 386 or 486 computer with a minimum of two megabytes of RAM. If you don't need expanded memory, this is the best CONFIG.SYS file for MS-DOS 5.0. Don't use this file if you're running Windows 3.1 unless you have a minimum of four megabytes of RAM:

```
device=C:\DOS\HIMEM.SYS /machine:1
DOS=high,UMB
buffers=20
files=20
break=on
shell=C:\COMMAND.COM C:\ /p
device=C:\DOS\SMARTDRV.SYS 512 256
device=C:\DOS\EMM386.EXE noems
devicehigh=C:\DOS\SETVER.EXE
devicehigh=C:\DOS\ANSI.SYS
lastdrive=z
^Z
```

SMARTDRV.SYS 512 256   creates a disk cache, using 512K of extended memory, which will decrease from 512K to 256K if another program needs the memory that SMARTDRV.SYS is occupying. A disk cache can dramatically increase hard-drive performance by using memory to buffer frequently accessed hard-drive data. When using MS-DOS 6.0, SMARTDRV.EXE is loaded by the AUTOEXEC.BAT file to enable disk caching. When SMARTDRV.EXE is loaded by the CONFIG.SYS file, it's used only for double buffering, which is a way of helping some hard drive controllers to communicate with memory controlled by EMM386.EXE (upper-memory-area manager). The correct format would be device=C:\DOS\SMARTDRV.EXE /double_buffer.

EMM386.EXE   is an upper-memory-area manager and expanded-memory emulator that will convert extended memory to expanded memory and allow the DEVICEHIGH and LOADHIGH commands to relocate some device drivers and programs into the HMA. The RAM switch enables expanded memory support and a partial amount of the upper-memory area in which device drivers can be loaded.

SETVER.EXE   loads an MS-DOS version table into memory, which allows applications not written for DOS 5.0 or 6.0 to think they're operating with a different version of DOS. The SETVER command, used at the DOS prompt, is used to display or modify the version table.

Lastdrive=z   is used to enable the use of all drive letters after the default of drive F:.

ANSI.SYS Some programs use ANSI escape sequences to control cursor movement, reassign the keyboard keys, and display graphics. The ANSI.SYS device driver must be loaded for these programs to function properly.

NOEMS This switch tells EMM386.EXE to allocate the upper memory area for device drivers that are loaded high with the DEVICEHIGH command. The advantage is more conventional memory, but no expanded memory will be available with this configuration. The NOEMS switch makes more upper memory available for device drivers than the RAM switch.

The following is a CONFIG.SYS file for when you're using DOS 5.0 or 6.0 and Windows 3.1 on a 386 or 486 computer with four megabytes of RAM:

```
device=C:\DOS\HIMEM.SYS
DOS=high,UMB
shell=C:\COMMAND.COM C:\ /p
device=C:\DOS\SMARTDRV.SYS 768 256
buffers=20
files=20
break=on
^Z
```

I don't recommend running Windows 3.1 with less than four megabytes of RAM. It will run with two megabytes, but its applications will run poorly. The Windows 3.1 setup program installs SMARTDRV.EXE in the AUTOEXEC.BAT file, replacing the SMARTDRV.SYS in the CONFIG.SYS file.

Here's a CONFIG.SYS file for after you've upgraded from MS-DOS 5.0 to MS-DOS 6.0 and run MEMMAKER:

```
DEVICE=C:\DOS\HIMEM.SYS /machine:1
DEVICE=C:\DOS\EMM386EXE RAM highscan
buffers=15,0
files=30
DOS=UMB
lastdrive=z
FCBS=4,0
DOS=high
break=on
shell=C:\COMMAND.COM C:\ /p
devicehigh /1:2,12048 =C:\DOS\SETVER.EXE
stacks=9,256
^Z
```

The MS-DOS 6.0 MEMMAKER utility optimizes memory usage by modifying parameters of command statements in the CONFIG.SYS file. If you ever get the error message *Stack Overflow*, use STACKS=9,256 as in the previous example.

Device=C:\DOS\VDISK.SYS 384 512 128 /e RAM disk in extended memory (MS-DOS 3.1 and 3.21).

Device=C:\DOS\RAMDRIVE.SYS 384 512 128 /e RAM disk in extended memory (MS-DOS 3.3 through 5.0).

Numlock=on Turns the numlock key on when the computer is booted (MS-DOS 6.0)

Numlock=off Turns the numlock key off when the computer is booted.

EDIT is a full-page ASCII text-editing program that's located in the DOS directory after you've installed MS-DOS 5.0 or 6.0. EDIT was available beginning with MS-DOS 5.0 and is a major improvement over the line editor EDLIN, which is included in all versions of MS-DOS except MS-DOS 6.0. EDIT has more capability than is required to use this book, so, to keep things simple, I'll describe only the simplest method of using EDIT.

Starting EDIT with the filename you want to edit loads that file automatically (you must have a path to the \DOS directory). For instance, type the command:

EDIT CONFIG.SYS

at the **C:\>** prompt to modify your CONFIG.SYS file with EDIT. Figure 26-2 shows a file you can easily modify by moving the cursor with the arrow keys, using the Insert and Delete keys, and typing the changes. To save the edited file and overwrite the old one:

1. Tap the Alt key.
2. Tap the F key.
3. Tap the X key.
4. Tap the Y key.

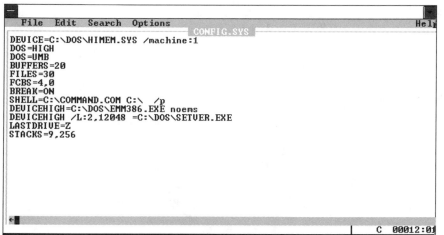

```
 File   Edit   Search   Options                              Help
                        CONFIG.SYS
DEVICE=C:\DOS\HIMEM.SYS /machine:1
DOS=HIGH
DOS=UMB
BUFFERS=20
FILES=30
FCBS=4,0
BREAK=ON
SHELL=C:\COMMAND.COM C:\  /p
DEVICEHIGH=C:\DOS\EMM386.EXE noems
DEVICEHIGH /L:2,12048 =C:\DOS\SETVER.EXE
LASTDRIVE=Z
STACKS=9,256




←
                                             C   00012:01
```

26-2
Editing a CONFIG.SYS file using the EDIT utility that comes with MS-DOS 5.0 and 6.0.

To discard changes and not overwrite the old file:

1. Tap the Alt key.
2. Tap the F key.
3. Tap the X key.
4. Tap the N key.

If you need help using EDIT, press the F1 function key. If you want to use the drop-down menu at the top of the screen, tap the Alt key and then the first letter of the word. For example, Alt–F will get you the File menu.

27 AUTOEXEC .BAT

The AUTOEXEC.BAT file is the second file that's automatically executed when the computer is turned on. If this file is absent from the root directory, you'll get a request for the time and date. If the AUTOEXEC.BAT file is in the root directory, the computer will skip the time and date request and begin executing the commands in the file. You can add the TIME and DATE commands to the AUTOEXEC.BAT file if you want to make these entries. See FIG. 27-1 for an explanation of the name AUTOEXEC.BAT.

27-1
The meaning of the AUTOEXEC.BAT filename and extension.

Normally, you use the AUTOEXEC.BAT file to set up the system parameters with DOS commands like PROMPT and PATH. You can also use it to execute programs, change drives, and change directories in what's called the batch-processing mode. Simply stated, each command in the file is executed in succession.

Why have an AUTOEXEC. BAT file?

- COPY CON means *copy from console* (p. 58).
- The .BAT extension designates a batch file (p. 40).
- You can run a batch file by typing the filename.
- The PROMPT PG command makes the current directory visible in the prompt (p. 55).
- The PATH command creates a route to specified directories, and enables execution of the .COM, .EXE, and .BAT files in those directories from any other directory (p. 89).

Making the AUTOEXEC. BAT file

Before making your AUTOEXEC.BAT file, you must make sure that your current directory is the root directory. Remember that the AUTOEXEC.BAT file must be in the root directory for it to be executed immediately after the computer is booted. First, use the PROMPT command to make the current directory visible by typing:

```
PROMPT $P$G
```

and Enter. If your prompt is anything other than **C:\>**, type CD \ and Enter. Your root directory is now your current directory. Now check to see if an AUTOEXEC.BAT file already exists by typing:

```
DIR AUTOEXEC.BAT
```

and Enter. If an AUTOEXEC.BAT file already exists, using the COPY CON command will replace the old AUTOEXEC.BAT file with your new one. MS-DOS 5.0 and 6.0 automatically create an AUTOEXEC.BAT file when they're installed, so be careful not to overwrite it. (To change an existing AUTOEXEC.BAT using MS-DOS 5.0 or 6.0, see the section *Using EDIT (MS-DOS 5.0 and 6.0)* in chapter 26—just substitute AUTOEXEC.BAT for CONFIG.SYS.)

If no AUTOEXEC.BAT file appears in the directory listing, use the COPY CON command to make an experimental AUTOEXEC.BAT file. At the **C:\>** prompt, type:

```
COPY CON AUTOEXEC.BAT
```

and Enter. Now type the following lines, ending each one by hitting the Enter key:

```
path=C:\;C:\DOS
time
date
prompt $p$g
C:\DOS\SMARTDRV.EXE
cd \names
type JOHN.DOC
cd \
^Z
```

(Use the C:\DOS\SMARTDRV.EXE command only if you're using DOS 6.0.)
Now, use the DIR command to be sure the AUTOEXEC.BAT file was created.

To get a better understanding of how the file operates, let's look at each line in the AUTOEXEC.BAT file you just made.

How AUTOEXEC. BAT operates

Path C:\;C:\DOS   This command sets a path to the root and then the \DOS directory of drive C:. This allows you to run any executable file in the root and \DOS directories without regard to which drive or directory you're in (the current drive or directory).

Time   This command shows the current time and asks you to enter a new time. If the current time is correct, hit the Enter key to continue.

Date   The DATE command works like the TIME command.

Prompt PG   This command changes the **C>** prompt to include the current directory. If you're in the root directory, the prompt will look like this: C:\>. If the \NAMES directory is the current directory, the prompt would look like this: C:\NAMES>.

C:\DOS\SMARTDRV.EXE (MS-DOS 6.0 only)   SMARTDRV.EXE is a disk-drive-caching program. It greatly enhances disk-drive performance. For detailed information, type: HELP SMARTDRV and Enter. You can also load SMARTDRV.EXE with the CONFIG.SYS file, but then it's used for double buffering (p. 127).

cd \names   This changes the current directory from the root directory to the \NAMES directory.

Type JOHN.DOC   The computer will type the contents of the JOHN.DOC file, which is in the \NAMES directory, to the monitor.

**cd **   The computer will change from the \NAMES directory back to the root directory, making the root directory current.

You can execute your AUTOEXEC.BAT file by rebooting the computer or typing the filename, AUTOEXEC. Type the filename and hit Enter to run the experimental AUTOEXEC.BAT file and watch the commands on the monitor as they execute.

Now that you know how the AUTOEXEC.BAT file works, below is a basic file that you can make and modify to suit your needs:

Another AUTOEXEC. BAT file

```
path C:\;C:\DOS
prompt $p$g
\mouse\mouse
^Z
```

The line \mouse\mouse loads a mouse-driver program into memory by executing the file MOUSE.COM in the \MOUSE directory. If you're using MS-DOS 5.0 or 6.0, you can load the mouse driver into the UMA (upper-memory area (p. 000) if you've created the proper CONFIG.SYS file, by substituting the following line:

```
loadhigh \mouse\mouse
```

Running a program with AUTOEXEC. BAT

You can use your AUTOEXEC.BAT file to start up a program once it has finished executing the rest of its commands. The following AUTOEXEC.BAT file will run WordPerfect 5.1 and change back to the root directory when you leave WordPerfect:

```
path C:\;C:\DOS
prompt $p$g
\mouse\mouse
cd \WP51
WP
cd \
^Z
```

It's not very likely, but if you accidentally put something weird in the AUTOEXEC.BAT file, you could create a looping situation or even lock up your computer. If either of these happen to you, you'll need to boot your system using a DOS system disk, and then replace or delete the AUTOEXEC.BAT file in the root directory of drive C:.

If you're using MS-DOS 6.0, you can avoid loading a faulty AUTOEXEC.BAT file. Simply press the reset button and, when the message *Starting MS-DOS . . .* appears, press the F5 function key and the AUTOEXEC.BAT as well as CONFIG.SYS files will be bypassed. In MS-DOS 6.0 lingo, this is termed a *clean boot*.

How to load software

You can load software onto the hard drive in many different ways. The programmers who develop software programs are responsible for the methods used to load it. The big problem is that there's no one standard.

- A directory is an area of a disk that separates related files from unrelated files (p. 38).
- The CONFIG.SYS file loads information and device drivers into memory when booting the system (p. 124).
- The AUTOEXEC.BAT file executes commands automatically when booting the system (p. 131).
- The CONFIG.SYS and AUTOEXEC.BAT files must be in the root directory.

What you should already know

You should have no problem loading software that comes with good documentation. Just follow the instruction manual provided with the software.

Software with instructions

First of all, be careful! Some cheap software programs will overwrite your existing AUTOEXEC.BAT or CONFIG.SYS files located in the root directory of your hard drive. This can change the operation of your system. Popular professional programs will usually ask you if you want to modify the AUTOEXEC.BAT or CONFIG.SYS files and that's okay. To be safe, you can make a \BAT directory on the C: drive and copy your AUTOEXEC.BAT and

No instructions

CONFIG.SYS files into it. If something happens to overwrite the originals, you can always copy them back to the root directory.

Software installation files

If you don't have the installation manual, look at the directory of files on the disk(s) of software you want to load and locate a file that seems to be an installation or setup file. It might look like one of the following:

```
SETUP.EXE
INSTALL.EXE
INSTALL.BAT
INSTALHD.BAT
HINSTALL.BAT
GO.BAT
START.BAT
```

Files with a .BAT extension are batch files, which run when you type the filename minus the .BAT extension. Like the AUTOEXEC.BAT file, they generally contain a list of commands that modify system parameters and then execute a main program file. It's a good idea to use the TYPE command to print out the batch file to see what it does. The following file is only a simple example of an installation file. If you had such a file on a disk in your A: drive and typed:

```
TYPE INSTALL.BAT
```

and Enter at the **A:** prompt, you might see a file like the following:

```
ECHO     ****************************************************************
ECHO     EXAMPLE SOFTWARE INSTALLATION PROGRAM
ECHO     ****************************************************************
MD C:\BOOK
MD C:\LEARN
COPY A:\BOOK C:\BOOK
COPY A:\LEARN C:\LEARN
```

Looking at the contents of this INSTALL.BAT file, you'll see that running the file will make two directories on hard drive C:, \BOOK and \LEARN. It will then copy the entire directories of \BOOK and \LEARN from drive A: to \BOOK and \LEARN on drive C:. What if the following line:

```
COPY A:\ C:\
```

was in the INSTALL.BAT file? This command statement will copy all the files in the root directory of drive A: to the root directory of drive C:. You must ask yourself if you want to copy software files into the root directory of drive C: and, if you do, will any existing files be replaced?

I wouldn't run the INSTALL.BAT file if it contained such a command statement because you should have only the necessary COMMAND.COM,

CONFIG.SYS, AUTOEXEC.BAT, and system files in the root directory of drive C:, along with software programs in their separate directories.

Compiled installation programs

Using the TYPE command won't give you a readable listing of a file with the extension .EXE or .COM because these files have been compiled, which converts them to machine language. For this reason, there's no way to know what these files will do until you run them.

I've evaluated many popular software programs with .EXE and .COM installation files and have found them all safe to run. To run an install program with an .EXE or .COM extension, just type the filename minus the extension.

Sometimes you need to add a drive letter to the filename in a command statement. If this is necessary, a message will be displayed on the monitor screen explaining what parameters are required to perform the installation. If you're asked if it's okay for the installation program to modify the AUTOEXEC.BAT or CONFIG.SYS, you should answer yes.

Two installation examples

Someone just gave you the original Lotus 1-2-3 program on floppy disks, but forgot to give you the manual. The first thing to do is go to drive A: and use the DIR command to find an installation file on the disk. You'll find a file with the name INSTALL.EXE. Start the install program with the following command:

INSTALL and Enter at the **A:\\)** prompt. You'll see displayed a set of options. Pick First Time installation and simply follow the onscreen instructions. If you're installing an early version of Lotus 1-2-3, you can also make a directory on your hard drive, copy all the program files into the directory, and then run the installation program from your hard drive. The following example shows how to use this procedure. First, make the directory C:\\123 by typing:

```
MD\123
```

and Enter at the **C:\\)** prompt. Now copy the files from the floppy disks to the \\123 directory with:

```
COPY a:\*.* C:\123
```

and Enter. When all the files are copied from the first disk, insert the next disk and hit the F3 function key. This will repeat the last command, which in this case is COPY A:*.* C:\123. Repeat this process until all the files from all the disks have been copied into the \\123 directory. Now change to the \\123 directory so it's the current directory by typing:

```
CD \123
```

and enter. The INSTALL.EXE program in Lotus 1-2-3 performs two operations; it installs and configures the software. Not all installation programs operate this way. To install some software programs, you must copy the files into a directory and then run a configuration program.

Because you already have Lotus 1-2-3 program files in the \123 directory, you can run the installation program to configure the software. Start the installation program by typing:

```
INSTALL
```

and Enter at the **C:\123>** prompt. The options menu will be displayed and, rather than pick First Time Installation, select Change Equipment. You'll then be prompted to enter the type of monitor and printer(s) you'll be using with Lotus 1-2-3. Don't worry about making a mistake. You can always rerun the installation program and change your entries.

Configuration

Most software programs need to be configured. When you configure a software program, you're asked what type of monitor and printer is connected to your computer system. The configuration program usually creates a CONFIG.DAT file (data file) using the information you enter in response to its questions. This information is then used to select the proper drivers for your monitor and printer.

A couple of configuration programs are NMCONFIG.EXE in Newsmaster and PBSETUP.EXE in Microsoft Paintbrush. Examples of installation and configuration programs combined into one program are INSTALL.EXE in Lotus 1-2-3, SETUP.EXE in Microsoft Windows, and VPPREP.EXE in Ventura Publisher.

Some software packages allow you to configure only during installation to the hard drive, such as Ventura Publisher. If you decide to use another printer or change monitor types, you must start the installation process of these software programs from drive A: using the original disks.

Some software packages are designed to be configured during program execution, such AutoCAD. After the installation is complete, you have to change to the \ACAD directory and type ACAD to execute the ACAD.EXE file. You must then choose Configure AutoCAD from the menu and follow the prompts to select your equipment.

Loading a software program that doesn't run

If you load a software program and it doesn't run correctly, or if the hard drive runs momentarily and then the screen goes blank, you more than likely need to run its configuration program. The reason the screen goes blank is that your monitor can't display anything when the software is configured with the wrong monitor driver.

HELP

MS-DOS 5.0 introduced the HELP command, which displays a brief description about DOS commands and is available from the command line. New, with MS-DOS 6.0, is a complete Command Reference Manual for all MS-DOS 6.0 commands that includes notes and examples about each command.

- The DIR command will list the files in the current directory (default) unless you specify other parameters (p. 51).
- Typing PROMPT PG will enable you to see the current directory in the prompt (p. 55).
- The DISKCOPY command is used to duplicate disks (p. 99).
- A forward slash / is used as a switch to activate alternate parameters available with a command (p. 41).

What you should already know

The information in this section pertains to the HELP command found in MS-DOS version 5.0.

MS-DOS 5.0 HELP

HELP *or* /?

The command

There are two ways to use the HELP command. You can type HELP followed by the command you want help about, or you can type the command

How to use 5.0 HELP

followed by the /? switch. Either method displays the same help information screen. Try it now; from the **C:\>** drive, type:

```
HELP DIR or DIR /?
```

and Enter. You'll be given a short description of the command, the syntax (the proper format of the command, including file and path specifications and any parameters or switches), and a description of all the parts of the command.

As you'll see from the screen display, even a simple command can appear complex and confusing. Even though you might not understand everything in the help screen, there is valuable information about switches that might save you the inconvenience of looking elsewhere. Now look at the help screen for the PROMPT command. Type:

```
HELP PROMPT or PROMPT /?
```

and Enter. The help screen will display a large list of options that modify what's displayed in the prompt. Some of this information won't be useful for the beginner, and might actually cause confusion. Try one more HELP command. Find out more about the DISKCOPY command with:

```
HELP DISKCOPY or DISKCOPY /?
```

and Enter. When you use a command that you've listed with the HELP command, keep in mind that information enclosed in square brackets is optional, so don't type the brackets. You can type HELP by itself and you'll see a list of the many DOS commands, with a brief description of what they do.

MS-DOS 6.0

Many changes to the HELP command make it necessary to describe it separately from the MS-DOS 5.0 version of HELP.

The commands   HELP, FASTHELP, or /?

How to use 6.0 HELP   The HELP command activates the Command Reference Manual. Type HELP and Enter at the **C:\>** prompt, and you'll see the Help menu, as shown in FIG. 29-1. From this menu, you can get detailed information, syntax, notes, and examples of how each command is used. Use the Tab key to move the cursor to the desired command and then press the Enter key. You can even get help about using HELP by pressing the F1 function key. What could be easier than that!

Now that I think about it, there is something easier. You can skip the Help Menu screen and go directly to the command, in the Command Reference Manual, by typing HELP followed by the command you want information about. Suppose you wanted HELP about the HELP command. Type:

```
HELP HELP
```

and Enter, and the help information in FIG. 29-2 will appear.

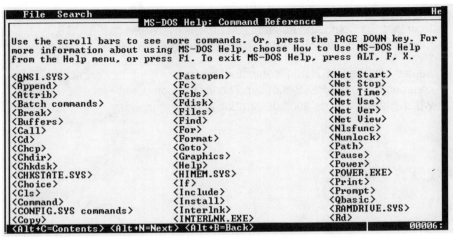

29-1 *The main menu of the MS-DOS Command Reference Manual.*

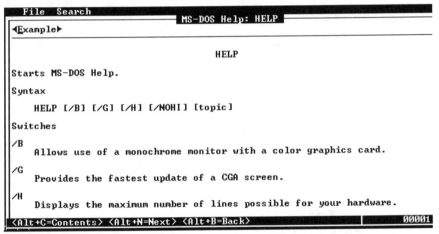

29-2 *Information on the Help command from the MS-DOS Command Reference Manual.*

The FASTHELP command replaces the MS-DOS 5.0 HELP command. There are two ways to use the FASTHELP command. You can type FASTHELP followed by the command you want help about, or you can type the command followed by the /? switch. Either method displays the same brief help information screen. Try it now; type:

```
FASTHELP DIR or DIR /?
```

and Enter. As you can see, all that information can be a little overwhelming. Now that the Command Reference Manual is available in MS-DOS 6.0, there's very little reason for the novice to use the FASTHELP command.

Remember, the FASTHELP command displays only a brief description of the command, and the HELP command opens the Command Reference Manual, which gives a very detailed description of the command.

30 MEM

Use the MEM command to check the status of the RAM in your computer.

- Specifying `PATH=C:\DOS` will allow you to execute the MEM.EXE file located in the \DOS directory from any drive or directory (p. 89).
- RAM is the main memory (workspace) in your computer. It consists of conventional memory (the first 640K) and extended memory (all memory above 640K) (p. 43).
- The HMA is the first 64K of memory immediately after one megabyte of RAM (p. 41).

What you should already know

MEM

The command

The MEM command was introduced with MS-DOS 4.01. MEM.EXE resides in the \DOS directory and can be executed from any drive or directory as long as there's a PATH to the \DOS directory. Type the command:

Using the MEM command

```
PATH=C:\DOS
```

and Enter.

Let's assume your computer is operating with MS-DOS 5.0 or 6.0, with two megabytes of RAM and the operating system loaded in the HMA with no EMS (expanded-memory specification) driver loaded. Type the MEM command and you'll see something like the following:

Situation one

```
 655360 bytes total conventional memory
 655360 bytes available to MS-DOS
 617696 largest executable program size

1048576 bytes total contiguous extended memory
      0 bytes available contiguous extended memory
 983040 bytes available XMS memory
        MS-DOS resident in High Memory Area
```

According to the above MEM listing, the computer has:

- 655,360 bytes of total conventional (base) memory
- 655,360 bytes of base memory available for MS-DOS to use
- 617,696 bytes, after DOS is loaded, available to run software
- 1,048,576 bytes total extended memory in the computer
- 0 bytes of extended memory available because HIMEM.SYS (the extended-memory manager) has taken control of the extended memory
- 983,040 bytes available under the control of HIMEM.SYS

Situation two Now assume that EMM386.SYS (MS-DOS 4.01) or EMM386.EXE (MS-DOS 5.0 and 6.0) was loaded in the CONFIG.SYS file of the previous example. After typing MEM at the DOS prompt, you'll see:

```
 655360 bytes total conventional memory
 655360 bytes available to MS-DOS
 622608 largest executable program size

 655360 bytes total EMS memory
 262144 bytes free EMS memory

1048576 bytes total contiguous extended memory
      0 bytes available contiguous extended memory
 622592 bytes available XMS memory
        MS-DOS resident in High Memory Area
```

The memory listing now shows 262,144 bytes of expanded memory (EMS) available for program usage.

MEM-command switches If you're absorbing the information in this book easily, you might be interested in a more detailed memory listing. Try the /c switch; type:

```
MEM /c
```

and Enter, and you'll see a display similar to the following:

```
Conventional Memory :

Name                 Size in Decimal          Size in Hex

----------           --------------------     ----------
MSDOS                16272      ( 15.9K)       3F90
HIMEM                 1184      (  1.2K)       4A0
SMARTDRV             21024      ( 20.5K)       5220
```

```
EMM386              8400      (  8.2K)         20D0
COMMAND             2688      (  2.6K)          A80
PROX              107792      (105.3K)        1A510
WP                381120      (372.2K)        5D0C0
COMMAND             2800      (  2.7K)          AF0
FREE                  64      (  0.1K)           40
FREE              113648      (111.0K)        1BBF0

Total  FREE :     113712      (111.0K)

Upper Memory :

Name                Size in Decimal        Size in Hex

------------        ----------------------  -----------
SYSTEM            180224      (176.0K)        2C000
STACKER            42336      ( 41.3K)         A560
MOUSE              13616      ( 13.3K)         3530
FREE               25872      ( 25.3K)         6510

Total  FREE :      25872      ( 25.3K)

Total bytes available to programs
  (Conventional+Upper) :                  139584    (136.3K)
Largest executable program size :         113456    (110.8K)
Largest available upper memory block :     25872    ( 25.3K)

1048576 bytes total contiguous extended memory
      0 bytes available contiguous extended memory
 289792 bytes available XMS memory
        MS-DOS resident in High Memory Area
```

For more advanced memory information (if using DOS 5.0 or 6.0), you can see information about other switches by using the HELP command. Type:

```
HELP MEM
```

and press the Enter key.

31 MS-DOS 6.0 utilities

Microsoft Corporation, the company that produces MS-DOS, has integrated a number of utilities written by other software companies into MS-DOS 6.0—utilities that will make your computing easier and more efficient.

What you should already know

- The CONFIG.SYS file loads information and device drivers into memory when you boot the system (p. 124).
- The AUTOEXEC.BAT file executes commands automatically when you boot the system (p. 131).
- The CONFIG.SYS and AUTOEXEC.BAT files must be in the root directory of drive C:.
- The .BAT extension designates a batch file (p. 40).
- You can run a batch file by typing the filename.

Brief descriptions

Clean boot   Allows you to control which files or commands load when you push the F5 or F8 function keys at bootup when the *Starting MS-DOS . . .* message appears.

DoubleSpace   Automatic software compression program that yields approximately two times the space on your hard drive.

MemMaker   Automatic memory-management program that configures your computer for optimum memory usage by moving device drivers and other memory-resident programs from base (conventional) memory to the UMA.

Anti-Virus   A program that can detect and remove over 1,000 different viruses from your computer system.

Vsafe   A program that protects your computer from being infected with a virus from an outside source.

Defragmenter   Makes files contiguous on your hard disk for better hard-drive performance.

Interlink   A program that allows the transfer of files between two computers with a serial cable.

Power Manager   A program that saves battery power on your notebook computer.

The following detailed descriptions should enable you to understand and use MS-DOS 6.0 utilities for increased performance and, if you're like me, a lot of fun.

Detailed information

Clean Boot was designed to allow you to more easily troubleshoot your computer's configuration by bypassing the loading of the CONFIG.SYS and AUTOEXEC.BAT files.

Clean Boot

To prevent the CONFIG.SYS and AUTOEXEC.BAT files from loading (similar to booting with a boot disk in drive A:) simply hold down the F5 function key while the computer is booting and the message *Starting MS-DOS . . .* is displayed on the screen. Pressing the F8 key while your computer is booting and the *Starting MS-DOS . . .* message is displayed enables you to choose which lines in the CONFIG.SYS file you want to load and whether or not you want to load the AUTOEXEC.BAT file. You can also add a question mark after a command and before the = sign in the CONFIG.SYS file, while booting, to be prompted whether or not you want the command loaded. For example:

```
(DEVICE?=C:\DOS\HIMEM.SYS)
```

DoubleSpace is a disk-compression program. More accurately, it's a software compression program that works automatically. It creates a file that looks and acts like a disk drive (C:, D:, E:, etc.). With DoubleSpace (DBLSPACE) activated, software copied or saved to your hard drive is first compressed. When you retrieve data or run a program, it's expanded to its normal state and made available for you to work with.

DoubleSpace

There are some things you must do before you run DBLSPACE to be sure it runs smoothly. First run CHKDSK to identify and remove any lost allocation units, with the command:

```
CHKDSK /f
```

at the **C:\>** prompt. If you get the message *Change lost allocation units to files [Y,N]*, press the letter N and the lost allocation units will be gone. In case you're wondering, a lost allocation unit is part of an open file that was unexpectedly interrupted before it was closed and stored on the hard drive with no name—therefore, it can't be accessed.

If there are no other error messages, you're ready to run DBLSPACE. Before you do, however, I'd like to say that it works well, but has a few drawbacks. First of all, when you compress a drive, you can't go back to the uncompressed drive. Secondly, if something goes wrong with the DBLSPACE file (the file that acts like a separate hard drive), all the software compressed into that file will be lost. Thirdly, you must have a CONFIG.SYS file containing the proper DoubleSpace device-driver command on your boot disk, or the DoubleSpace drive won't be available. If you are a DOS beginner , I recommend that you don't run DBLSPACE.

To run DBLSPACE, type the command DBLSPACE and Enter at the **C:\>** prompt. The program will give you three choices, setup DBLSPACE, learn about DBLSPACE, and Quit. I recommend pressing the F1 function key to learn about the program before doing the setup.

MemMaker

You must have an 80386 or 80486 processor to use MemMaker. Its purpose is to optimize and free base (conventional) memory by moving device drivers and memory-resident programs to the UMA. If you're running Windows 3.1, you'll want Windows to be able to use all the UMA, so I suggest that you don't use this program.

Before running MemMaker, load all memory-resident programs (TSRs). MemMaker will look to see what programs have been loaded and then attempt to move these programs to the UMA. To run MemMaker, type MEMMAKER and Enter at the **C:\>** prompt.

As usual, detailed help is available via the F1 function key. You can use the spacebar to select Express Setup. The next screen will ask if you use any programs that use expanded memory. Expanded memory is explained in chapter 8, *List of terms*, p. 000. Follow the program until it has completed its operation. Your CONFIG.SYS file will contain changes and additions to optimize your system.

Anti-Virus

Computer viruses will cause your computer to act differently. When infected, you might hear a strange noise, see a nasty message on the monitor screen, notice that some programs don't work. At their worst, computer viruses will totally disable your system and corrupt the hard drive. Whatever the cause, Microsoft Anti-Virus can locate these viruses for you and remove them from your computer's memory, hard disk, and floppy disks.

Use Anti-Virus as often as you feel necessary. You can't hurt anything by running it. Like a disease, you want to stop it as soon as possible. Your computer can't get a virus from the air like people, from an external source like a friend's disk, a network, or a BBS (bulletin board service).

If you don't yet have a path to \DOS, type:

```
PATH C:\DOS
```

and Enter. To start Anti-Virus, type MSAV and Enter. You'll see the Main Menu screen shown in FIG. 31-1. This program is simple to use. Pressing the F1 function key will provide easy-to-understand help. I put a disk containing an infected WP.EXE file into drive A: of my computer. I then used the Select New Drive option to pick drive A:, and the Detect option to scan for a virus. The message shown in FIG. 31-2 appeared. I then selected Clean to remove the virus from the WP.EXE file.

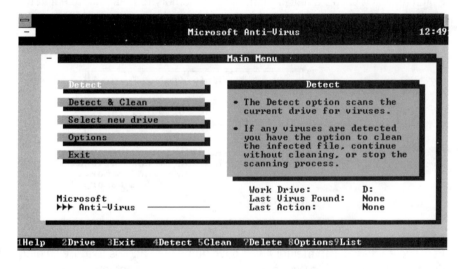

31-1
The Microsoft Anti-Virus Main Menu.

Be sure to select the Options selection from the Main Menu. Then press the F1 function key to learn about the different types of viruses and how to set up MSAV to detect and remove them.

Vsafe

Vsafe will detect a virus before it infects your computer system and should be loaded directly after bootup or placed in the AUTOEXEC.BAT file. If a virus attempts to infect your system, a warning message will appear on the screen, giving you a choice of stopping, continuing, or booting.

```
A:\WP.EXE

                         Main Menu

    Detect                              Detect
    Detect  -                                         100%
    Select    Virus Friday 13th  was found in: WP.EXE         1
    Option
    Exit          Clean     Continue      Stop      Delete    100%
                                                              3

                              Work Drive:        A:
    Microsoft                 Last Virus Found:  Friday 13th
    ▶▶▶ Anti-Virus ──────     Last Action:       None
```

31-2
The Microsoft Anti-Virus Main Menu, showing the Friday 13th virus found in a WP.EXE file.

VSAFE is a memory-resident or TSR (terminate and stay resident) program, which means it uses a small amount of base memory to make it immediately available with a predefined keystroke, such as Alt–V. To start VSAFE type VSAFE and Enter. You'll see the message shown in FIG. 31-3 on the screen.

```
┌─────────────────────────────────┐
│           USafe (tm)            │
│                                 │
│    Copyright (c) 1991-1992      │
│  Central Point Software, Inc.   │
│    Hotkey:    <Alt><U>          │
└─────────────────────────────────┘

USafe successfully installed.
USafe is using 23K of conventional memory,
          23K of XMS memory,
          0K of EMS memory.

C:\>_
```

31-3
Screen showing the VSAFE TSR resident and active.

Because a TSR stays in memory, you have immediate access to it. By holding down the Alt key and pressing the letter V, you have immediate access to the Vsafe options box (shown in FIG. 13-4), which allows you to change the way it works.

Suppose a friend gives you a nifty little program on a disk for you to try out. The Friday 13th virus is on the disk and, of course, your friend doesn't know it. You put it in your floppy drive and run the program, which allows the virus to infect the computer's memory. You like the program, but decide that you don't want to keep it, so you take the disk out of the drive and put it aside. You now run WordPerfect 5.1 and everything is fine, but unknown to you, the virus in memory has now infected the WP.EXE file. The next time you *try* to run WordPerfect 5.1, the screen goes blank and your computer stops functioning. Your first thought would probably be that something went

```
        VSafe Warning Options

    ┌─────────────────────────────┬────┐
    │  Warning type               │ ON │
    ├─────────────────────────────┼────┤
    │ 1 │ HD low-level format     │ X  │
    │ 2 │ Resident                │    │
    │ 3 │ General write-protect   │    │
    │ 4 │ Check executable files  │ X  │
    │ 5 │ Boot sector viruses     │ X  │
    │ 6 │ Protect HD boot sector  │ X  │
    │ 7 │ Protect FD boot sector  │    │
    │ 8 │ Protect executable files│    │
    └─────────────────────────────┴────┘

    Press 1-8 toggle ON/OFF
    Press <ESC> to Exit
    Press ALT-U to unload from memory
```

31-4
The VSAFE option box that appears when you press Alt–V.

wrong with the computer or the software, so you try running other programs and they also become infected.

Now let's use the same situation, only with VSAFE loaded. You insert your friend's disk into the floppy drive and run the nifty little program, only this time the warning box in FIG. 31-5 pops up on the screen. VSAFE is warning you that a virus has been found, and asks you to hit a key to take action. When you press a key, the Vsafe recommended action box will appear.

If you select Stop, the procedure you were initiating will stop so the virus can't infect the system. For example, I was trying to execute a file on a disk in drive A: that was infected with a virus and, when I selected Stop, I received the message *Access Denied*. If the infected file were allowed to execute, the virus would have spread to other areas of the computer.

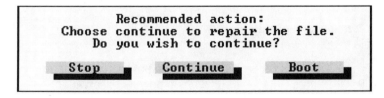

```
        Recommended action:
   Choose continue to repair the file.
        Do you wish to continue?

   ┌────────┐  ┌──────────┐  ┌────────┐
   │  Stop  │  │ Continue │  │  Boot  │
   └────────┘  └──────────┘  └────────┘
```

31-5
The VSAFE Recommended Action box.

If you select Continue, Vsafe will remove the virus from the file. If you select Boot, Vsafe will immediately boot the computer, thereby preventing infection by the virus.

Defragmenter

When you save files to a disk, they're written to the first available unoccupied areas of the disk. If each of those areas is small and the file being saved is large, then the file will become fragmented because it's occupying more than one location on the disk. The FAT (file-allocation table) stores the locations of these fragments. When the file is saved or retrieved, the drive must go to two or more locations, which takes more time. The more fragmented the file is, the longer it takes to save or retrieve.

The MS-DOS 6.0 defragmenter moves file fragments into a contiguous position, thereby increasing performance. Before running Defragmenter, it's wise to delete all unnecessary files and remove unwanted directories. Then run CHKDSK to remove any lost allocation units by typing:

```
CHKDSK /f
```

and Enter at the **C:** prompt. Run the Defragmenter by typing DEFRAG and Enter. You'll see the Defragmenter main screen, with a list of your systems drives to select from. You can continue to run the program, or press the F1 function key for help information. This program is very easy to use.

Interlink This is a program that links two computers together so you can copy files back and forth. A null-modem serial cable is connected to a serial port on each computer. Then each computer is set up as a server or client, depending on which direction the files are going.

Interlink is beyond the skills of the beginner, so I'll refer you to a very easy-to-use program called File Shuttle Express by GetC Software Inc., 800-663-8066. There are many other file-transfer programs on the market, but this one is my favorite because it's simple to understand and doesn't require a device driver.

Power Manager This program reduces power consumption by monitoring software applications and your computer's hardware devices. Power Manager was designed mainly for notebook computers using battery power.

This program has three power settings—Max, Reg, and Min—and is loaded into extended memory (uses about 5K) by the CONFIG.SYS file. The STD switch turns on hardware power management if your computer supports advanced power management (APM). Add one of the following to your CONFIG.SYS file to use Power Manager:

```
DEVICE=C:\DOS\POWER.EXE ADV:MAX (maximum power conservation)
DEVICE=C:\DOS\POWER.EXE ADV:REG (average power conservation)
DEVICE=C:\DOS\POWER.EXE ADV:MIN (least power conservation)
DEVICE=C:\DOS\POWER.EXE STD      (APM)
```

When one of the previous devices is loaded, typing POWER at the prompt will give the status of the CPU, as follows:

```
Power Management Status

Setting = ADV: MAX
CPU: idle 92% of time
```

32 DR DOS 6.0

DR DOS is a disk operating system by Digital Research Corporation. MS-DOS and DR DOS commands are very similar. Because MS-DOS is the leader in the DOS world, Digital Research Corporation has fashioned their DOS after MS-DOS. If you can use MS-DOS, you can effectively use DR DOS. DR DOS 5.0 and 6.0 have some new commands and enhancements that aren't available in MS-DOS 6.0.

What you should already know

- MS-DOS is a product of Microsoft, and is the most popular disk operating system.
- Using the /? switch after a command will display help information for that command (p. 139).
- The CONFIG.SYS file modifies the operating-system defaults at bootup (p. 124).
- The AUTOEXEC.BAT file is a batch file that enables you to execute a series of commands (p. 131).
- You can use the XCOPY command to copy a directory along with its files and subdirectories to another directory or drive (p. 118).

DR DOS 6.0 installation

One very important thing about DR DOS 6.0 is how easy it is to install. I installed it on a 386 computer that already had MS-DOS 4.01 on its hard drive. It took some time, probably because I installed every option, but the installation was flawless, very logical, and easy to follow.

RENDIR   RENDIR allows you to rename a directory. Suppose you have a \LOTUS directory that contains five subdirectories and you want it to have the directory name \123 instead. You could use MS-DOS's XCOPY command to copy the \LOTUS directory to the \123 directory, delete all the files, and then remove the subdirectories from the \LOTUS directory, or you can use the RENDIR command as follows:

```
RENDIR \LOTUS \123
```

MOVE   You can use the MOVE command to move a file, group of files, or directory structure to another drive or directory. Suppose you wrote some personal documents with the file extension .PER, in WordPerfect, and saved them on your hard drive. Then, for privacy reasons, you decide to keep them on a floppy disk instead of your hard drive. You could move them to the disk by typing:

```
MOVE C:\WP51\*.PER A:\
```

SECURITY   When you install DR DOS 6.0, you have the option to require a master password during bootup. I installed the password option and then tried to boot the system with a bootable disk only to discover that the computer wouldn't allow access to the hard drive. I had to modify the CONFIG.SYS file and copy it to the DR DOS 6.0 bootable disk before I could get in. This level of protection is good in order to keep the riff raff out of your computer, but, in my opinion, you should know a fair amount about DOS before you use this option.

DISKOPT (disk optimizer)   Use the DISKOPT command to defragment a hard drive. Fragmentation occurs when files are deleted and new files are written to the areas where deleted files previously existed. DISKOPT improves performance by making files contiguous.

DOSBOOK   DOSBOOK is a new command that opens an online book of DOS commands, so detailed help is instantly available. It's written in a hypertext format, which means that key words in the text that provide additional information are highlighted. If you place the cursor on the highlighted word and hit the Enter key, you'll see a description of that word or command.

Super PC-Kwik   This program creates a *disk cache*, which increases hard-drive performance by using RAM. When data is retrieved from the hard drive, a copy is placed into the part of RAM reserved for the disk cache. If the data is needed again, it's retrieved from RAM instead of the slower hard drive, which results in a dramatic boost in performance. Tests I've done with the Norton Utilities program show this disk cache to be the fastest. MS-DOS has a similar program that's loaded with the file SMARTDRV.SYS.

SuperStor   You can increase your hard-drive storage capacity by installing SuperStor during the installation process. After installation, run the

SSTOR.EXE file and follow the setup program, which will compress the data on the specified drive. Data is uncompressed and compressed automatically as it's read from and written to the disk. You should be able approximately double your storage space. I've noticed a small degradation in speed, so if you have a slow computer you might want to specify compressing only half of the existing drive. This way you'll have some uncompressed space for programs you want to run as fast as possible.

The following are other commands and enhancements available in earlier versions of DR DOS, as well as DR DOS 6.0:

FILELINK If you have two computers and each one has a serial port, you can use FILELINK to transfer files from one computer to the other when they're connected with an RS-232 null-modem serial cable. One computer is entered into slave mode and files are transferred from the master computer using the FILELINK TRANSMIT command at baud rates up to 115,200 bits per second.

XDEL You can use the XDEL command with the /s and /d switches to delete all the files in a directory and all its subdirectories, and then remove the directory and all its subdirectories. The XDEL command is a tremendous time and labor saver when removing large directory structures, because the alternative is to delete all the files in each subdirectory and then remove each subdirectory. The following is an example command:

```
XDEL \MONEY /s /d
```

Suppose the \MONEY directory had two subdirectories, \MONEY\DIMES and \MONEY\NICKELS. Using the example XDEL command statement above would completely remove \MONEY\DIMES, \MONEY\NICKELS, and \MONEY, as well as all files contained in them.

SCRIPT The SCRIPT command converts ASCII and Hewlett-Packard LaserJet II files to a PostScript file so it can be printed by a PostScript printer.

Conclusion

I personally think that DR DOS 6.0 is better than MS-DOS 5.0, and I recommend it highly. Now that MS-DOS 6.0 is available, however, the scales have balanced and I would hesitate leaving the massive installed base of MS-DOS users.

Appendices

A Loading DOS

The dealer who sold you your computer system probably formatted the hard drive and loaded the DOS files in a directory called DOS. If he didn't, you'll need to do it yourself. This appendix contains information on partitioning, formatting, and making a DOS directory on your hard drive.

DOS is the foundation for everything you do with your computer. It's important to have a path going to a DOS directory on your C: drive so that you have immediate access to all the wonderful external DOS commands not resident in COMMAND.COM. It's accepted practice to have a DOS directory on the C: drive, and it's essential to use this book effectively.

Why you load DOS

- The first floppy drive in your computer is drive A:.
- The hard drive (hard disk) in your computer is drive C:.
- The cursor is the blinking underscore on the screen.
- **A)** and **C)** are called prompts (p. 43.
- Booting is the process of turning on the computer, which loads the DOS system files and displays a prompt on the monitor (p. 37).
- The DOS system diskette is also called a DOS boot disk (p. 39).
- All disks must be formatted when new (p. 41).

What you should already know

Existing hard-drive conditions

You will have one of the four following conditions with a newly purchased computer:

- The hard drive in your system is DOS formatted and has a directory called DOS containing all the DOS programs. This is the end result you need to achieve. If you purchased your system from a local dealer, you probably have a DOS directory containing the DOS program files and you need go no further.
- The hard drive in your system is DOS formatted, but has no DOS directory containing DOS programs. You need to create a DOS directory and copy in the DOS program files.
- The hard drive in your system has been low-level formatted, but hasn't been DOS formatted and, therefore, has no DOS directory. You need to create a partition(s), format the partition(s), make a DOS directory, and copy the DOS program files into the DOS directory. If you purchased your system by mail order, you could be in this category.
- The hard drive in your system hasn't been low-level formatted and can't be used until this is done. The dealer who sold you your computer should have low-level formatted it. Take your system back to the dealer and ask him to low-level format the hard drive. All IDE hard drives come low-level formatted from the factory, so if you have one, you aren't in this category.

Creating a DOS partition

Is your hard drive formatted? First, find out if your system boots from the hard drive. Check the floppy drives and make sure there are no floppy disks in them. Now turn on the computer. If you see an error message like the following:

```
Drive not ready error
Insert BOOT diskette in drive A:
Press any key when ready
```

your hard drive probably hasn't been DOS formatted and, therefore, has no DOS directory. If your computer boots properly and you have a C> prompt on the monitor, then skip to a later section in this appendix, *Checking for the DOS directory*.

 Caution: If you have something other than a new computer, it's possible that it won't boot from the hard drive due to improper setup information or a missing COMMAND.COM program. Get assistance from a professional if this could be the case. Formatting the hard drive will erase all software on it. You shouldn't do this unless you're positive that the drive hasn't already been formatted with DOS.

Before you can DOS format your computer, you must create a DOS bootable partition with the FDISK.COM program on the DOS system disk. The following FDISK example is from MS-DOS 3.30. Earlier versions of DOS won't allow extended partitions and, therefore, allow you to format only a 32Mg hard drive (unless you're using third-party software). MS-DOS 4.01, 5.0, and

6.0 will allow up to 2,000-megabyte primary or extended partitions. Finally, the restrictions are gone!

Execute the FDISK.COM program, and create a partition by typing `FDISK` and Enter at the **A>**. You'll get a main menu screen similar to the following:

```
Fixed Disk Options

1. Create a DOS partition
2. Make a Partition Active
3. Delete a DOS Partition
4. Display Partition Data

   Enter Choice:[ ]
```

To make a partition, type 1 and Enter, and you'll see:

```
Current Fixed Disk Drive: 1

1. Create Primary DOS partition
2. Create Extended DOS partition

   Enter choice: [ ]
```

Type 1 again and Enter. If any partitions exist, you won't need to make any, so hit the Esc key a few times until you exit the program. If no partitions exist, you will get the following:

```
Create Primary DOS Partition

Current Fixed Disk Drive: 1

Do you wish to use the maximum size
for a DOS partition and make the DOS
partition active (Y/N).........? [ ]
```

If you have a hard disk that's 32 megabytes or less, answer Y. If you have a hard disk that's over 32 megabytes, answer N. If you're using MS-DOS 4.01, 5.0, or 6.0, you can answer Y if you want the full capacity of the hard drive to be the primary partition, drive C:; otherwise, answer N.

If you answered Y, the partition will be made and you'll be asked to restart the computer. If you answered N, there are more steps to complete. So let's use N for the following example, making partitions for a 64Mg hard drive. After answering N, you'll see the following:

```
Create Primary DOS Partition

Current Fixed Disk Drive: 1

Total disk space is 970 cylinders.
Maximum space available for partition
is 503 cylinders.

Enter partition size............: [503]
```

Hit the Enter key, and you'll see:

```
Create Primary DOS Partition

Current Fixed Disk Drive: 1

Partition Status      Type  Start  End Size
  C: 1                PRI DOS    1  503  503

Primary DOS partition created
```

Now, to create the extended DOS partition, hit the Esc key and you'll see:

```
Fixed Disk Options

1. Create a DOS partition
2. Make a Partition Active
3. Delete a DOS Partition
4. Display Partition Data

   Enter Choice:[ ]
```

Type 1 and Enter, and you'll see:

```
Create Primary DOS Partition

Current Fixed Disk Drive: 1

1. Create Primary DOS partition
2. Create Extended DOS partition

Enter choice: [ ]
```

Type 2 and Enter, and you'll see:

```
Create Extended DOS Partition

Current Fixed Disk Drive: 1

Partition Status      Type  Start  End Size
  C: 1                PRI DOS    1  503  503

Total disk space is 970 cylinders.
Maximum space available for partition
is 466 cylinders.

Enter partition size............: [466]
```

Hit the Enter key, and you'll see:

```
Create Extended DOS Partition

Current Fixed Disk Drive: 1

Partition Status      Type  Start  End Size
  C: 1                PRI DOS    1  503  503
     2                EXT DOS  504  969  466

Extended DOS partition created
```

Hit the Esc key and you'll see the following:

```
No logical drives defined

Total partition size is 466 cylinders.

Maximum space available for logical
drive is 466 cylinders.

Enter logical drive size........: [466]
```

Hit the Enter key and logical drive D: will be created, as shown:

```
Create Logical DOS Drive(s)

Drv Start End  Size
 D:  504  969  466

All available space in the Extended DOS
partition is assigned to logical drives.
```

Hit the Esc key to return to the FDISK Main Menu:

```
Fixed Disk Options

1. Create a DOS partition
2. Make a Partition Active
3. Delete a DOS Partition
4. Display Partition Data

   Enter Choice:[ ]

WARNING! No partitions marked active
```

Now you must make the primary partition active, so it can be DOS bootable, so type 2 and Enter, and you'll see:

```
Change Active Partition

Current Fixed Disk Drive: 1

Partition Status    Type  Start End Size
 C: 1               PRI DOS   1  503 503
    2               EXT DOS  504 969 466

Total disk space is 970 cylinders.
Enter the number of the partition you
want to make active............: [ ]
```

Type 1 and Enter, and you'll see:

```
Change Active Partition

Current Fixed Disk Drive: 1

Partition Status    Type  Start End Size
 C: 1        A      PRI DOS   1  503 503
    2               EXT DOS  504 969 466

Total disk space is 970 cylinders.

Partition 1 made active
```

Now push the Esc key to exit the FDISK program. Push the reset button to reboot the computer. Your hard drive is now ready for DOS formatting.

Formatting the hard drive

Boot the computer with the DOS system disk in drive A:. The following command will format the hard drive with the DOS system:

```
FORMAT C: /s
```

When you hit Enter, you'll see the following message:

```
WARNING, ALL DATA ON NON-REMOVABLE DISK
DRIVE C: WILL BE LOST!
Proceed with Format (Y/N)?
```

Type Y and Enter, and you'll be asked to enter a volume label. Just hit the Enter key. Formatting of drive C: will now begin. When the formatting is complete, the DOS system files and COMMAND.COM will be put on the hard drive, so it will boot up to the **C)** prompt.

If you created an extended partition, you'll need to format it before it can be used. It will be given the next available drive letter, D:. To format drive D:, type:

```
FORMAT D:
```

and Enter at the **A)** prompt. Now reboot the system by taking the floppy disk out of drive A: and hitting the reset button. When the computer boots, you'll be asked for the time and date. Hit the Enter key two times and you'll see a **C)** prompt on the monitor screen. Nice job!

Checking for the DOS directory

Read this section if your dealer formatted the hard drive and you don't know if you have a DOS directory, or if you have a DOS directory but don't know if it contains DOS program files.

Turn the computer on. You should get a **C)** prompt on the monitor screen. Now use the DIR command to list the files in the root directory. If the DOS directory exists, then look inside the directory to be sure the DOS files are there. Type:

```
DIR \DOS
```

and Enter. If the listing of the DOS directory scrolls through a bunch of filenames, the DOS program files have been installed for you. If the DOS directory exists, but is empty skip to the section *Copying the DOS program files into the DOS directory*.

If you can't find the DOS directory on the C: drive, the following instructions will explain how to make the DOS directory.

Create a DOS directory simply by typing MD \DOS and ENTER at the **C>** prompt.

If you're using MS-DOS 3.30, you'll have two 360K floppy disks. One is the system disk and the other contains DOS supplemental programs. Put the system disk in drive A:, and type the following:

```
COPY A:\*.* C:\DOS
```

and Enter. Now put the DOS supplemental programs disk into drive A: and type the following:

```
COPY A:\*.* C:\DOS
```

and Enter. If you're using DOS 4.01, simply locate the disks containing the DOS program files and copy them to the DOS directory (as was explained previously).

The files on the MS-DOS 5.0 disks are compressed, so you must use the installation program on disk 1 and go through the setup procedure to install the DOS program files.

If you check your DOS directory using the DIR command and see a listing of your DOS files, you did the procedure correctly. If you don't get the directory listing, go back to the section *Making the DOS directory* and try it again. More than likely you made a typing error. Now you're ready for the *DOS training* section of this book.

Other DOS commands

This book has defined and explained the most commonly used DOS commands. There are, however, many other DOS commands available from MS-DOS versions 3.21 to 6.0. Although I haven't described them in detail, they're listed below with a brief description of what they do:

Command	Description
APPEND	Like the PATH command, but searches for nonexecutable files in specified drives and directories
ASSIGN	Use to give a drive a different drive letter (not included, but works with MS-DOS 6.0).
ATTRIBUTE	Use to change read-only and archive file attributes
CALL	Calls one batch program from another batch program
CHCP	Selects DOS code pages
CHKDSK	Checks specified disk for errors and gives status
CHOICE	MS-DOS 6.0 only; used in a batch file to allow users to choose action with a specified keystroke.
CLS	Clears the monitor

Command	Description
COMMAND	Invokes a new command processor
COMP	Compares files or groups of files
COUNTRY	Selects the time, date, and currency formats for a foreign country; use in the CONFIG.SYS file
CTTY	Changes the way the system directs I/O
DEBUG	A binary editing program
DISKCOMP	Use to compare two floppy disks
DEVICE	Use in CONFIG.SYS to load a device driver
DISPLAY.SYS	Code-page switching for the video display
DOSKEY	Edits command lines, recalls MS-DOS commands, and creates macros (MS-DOS 5.0 and 6.0)
DOSSHELL	Starts the MS-DOS shell
DRIVER.SYS	Use in CONFIG.SYS to load drivers that bridge DOS with external devices
DRIVPARM	Use in CONFIG.SYS to change default device-driver configuration
ECHO	Turns the display of text in batch files on or off
EDIT	DOS 5.0 and 6.0 editor for editing ASCII files
EDLIN	A line editor used to create and edit ASCII files (not included, but works with MS-DOS 6.0)
EXPAND	File-uncompression command (MS-DOS 5.0 and 6.0)
ERASE	Use to remove (delete) files
EXE2BIN	Changes a file with .EXE extension to binary format
EXIT	Returns control to a previous command processor
FASTOPEN	Decreases the time necessary to reopen and close files
FC	Compares files and displays actual differences
FCBS	Use in CONFIG.SYS file to select the number of file-control blocks open at one time

FIND	Searches through a file for a specified string of text
GOTO	In a batch file, redirects execution to a label
GRAFTABL	Enables the display of extended character sets in graphics mode
GRAPHICS	Loads a driver to enable graphic screen dumps
GWBASIC	A type of BASIC programming language
IF	Performs conditional processing in batch programs
INSTALL	Use in CONFIG.SYS to execute FASTOPEN, KEYB, NLSFUNC, or SHARE
JOIN	Joins a disk drive with a directory (not included, but works with MS-DOS 6.0)
KEYB	Loads foreign-language keyboard characters
LABEL	Add, change, or delete a disk volume label
LASTDRIVE	Use in CONFIG.SYS file to specify the last drive letter the computer will recognize
LINK	Creates executable program files from object files
LOADFIX	Loads and runs a program above the first 64K of memory
PRINTER.SYS	Code-page switching for printing foreign fonts (not included with MS-DOS 6.0)
PRINT	Use to send a file to a printer
REN	Short for RENAME—use to change a filename
MEM	Displays current memory status
NLSFUNC	Use for loading country-specific information
MODE	Use to configure serial and printer ports, display mode, and keyboard mode; set code pages; and and redirect printing
PAUSE	Suspends processing of a batch file and displays a message
QBASIC	Starts the MS-DOS 5.0 and 6.0 QBasic programming environment

Command	Description
RECOVER	Use to recover an unreadable file or disk
RAMDRIVE.SYS	Load with CONFIG.SYS file to create a virtual disk
REM	Use in CONFIG.SYS or batch files to add remarks
REPLACE	Will replace files or add files to a disk
SELECT	Installs DOS using country-specific information
SET	Use to set and look at the command processor's environment
SHARE	Enables file sharing in a network environment
SHELL	Enables the use of another command processor
SHIFT	Shifts the position of replaceable parameters in batch files
SIZER	Used by MS-DOS 6.0 MemMaker to determine memory size of device drivers and TSRs.
SORT	Filters specific files from a group of mixed files
STACKS	Use in CONFIG.SYS to change number of stacks
SUBST	Substitutes a drive letter for a path
SYS	Use to transfer the DOS system to a hard or floppy disk
VDISK.SYS	Load with CONFIG.SYS file to create a virtual disk
VERIFY	Checks data written to a disk for integrity
VOL	Shows the volume label of a hard or floppy disk

About the author

Richard Cadway's involvement with computer systems began in 1980 when
he purchased an Atari 800 Computer System. He then mastered the BASIC
programming language and progressed into numerical-control programming.
Numerical-control programs direct the movement of cutters in machine tools
such as lathes and milling machines. Using a terminal and modem, he wrote
programs in California on an IBM 360 mainframe computer located in
Pennsylvania. He continued N/C programming using a Texas Instruments
Professional Computer System, which is very similar to the IBM PC computer.

Cadway has been a consultant since 1986, and he has built and sold
computer systems to people in all walks of life including engineers,
housewives, retirees, teachers, professionals, and other individuals, as well as
businesses. He has also built and installed local-area networks (LANs) using
Invisible, Lantastic, and Novell software with Arcnet, Ethernet, and
proprietary hardware.

While helping people understand and use his computer systems, he has
found that the majority of his customers don't want to learn the complete
DOS operating system. They want to learn only the DOS commands
necessary to use their computer software—programs such as WordPerfect,
Microsoft Word, Windows, Lotus 1-2-3, dBASE, and Ventura Publisher.